CAST-METAL SIGNS

an unsung history

written and photographed by

JOHN HANNAVY

First published in 2026 by
Whittles Publishing,
an imprint of Porto Press Ltd.
3 Connaught Road,
St Albans, AL3 5RX

All rights reserved. No part of this publication may be reproduced, stored in a retrieval system, or transmitted in any form or by any means, electronic, mechanical, photocopying, recording or otherwise,
without prior permission in writing from the publisher.
The author has made every effort to ensure the accuracy of information contained in this publication,
but assume no responsibility for any errors, inaccuracies, inconsistencies and omissions. Likewise, every
effort has been made to contact copyright holders. If any copyright material has been reproduced unwittingly and without permission the Publisher will gladly receive information enabling them to rectify any error or omission in subsequent editions.

Text, cover, page design and all photographs unless otherwise credited, copyright © 2026 John Hannavy

British Library Cataloguing in Publication Data
A CIP record for this book is available from the British Library

ISBN: 9781849956581

The rights of John Hannavy to be identified as the Author of this work has been asserted by him in accordance with the Copyright, Design and Patents Act 1988.

Printed and bound in Great Britain, using paper from responsible sources, by CPI Printing

To order please go to our website
www.whittlespublishing.com
or contact our distributor,
BookSource, 50 Cambuslang Road, Clydesmill Industrial Estate, Glasgow G32 8NB
Telephone 0141 642 9192

COVER IMAGE
One of the Millennium Mileposts erected across the National Cycle Network. Created by John Mills and cast by Taylor's Foundry Ltd, this one is in Calne, Wiltshire. There are three other designs, created by three different artists.

TITLE PAGE IMAGE
Edwardian cast-metal combined door knocker and letterbox. Letterboxes became popular shortly after Rowland Hill's 'penny post' was introduced in 1840.

CONTENTS PAGE IMAGES
top: The nameplate from Southern Railway 'Merchant Navy Class' locomotive No. 35029 *Ellerman Lines*.
bottom: Cast grey metal front badge from a 1920s Undertype Steam Lorry – so-called because the steam engine was mounted under the chassis – built by Garretts of Leiston, Suffolk. (*image: Brian Gooding*)

CONTENTS

INTRODUCTION 5

A LITTLE HISTORY 11

MAKING CAST-METAL SIGNS 35

OUT ON THE OPEN ROAD 51

ON THE WATER, AND BY THE WATER'S EDGE 73

RAILWAY SIGNAGE – NAMES, NUMBERS AND DIRECTIONS 87

SITES AND COLLECTIONS FEATURED IN THIS BOOK 119

ACKNOWLEDGEMENTS 126

FURTHER READING 127

INDEX 128

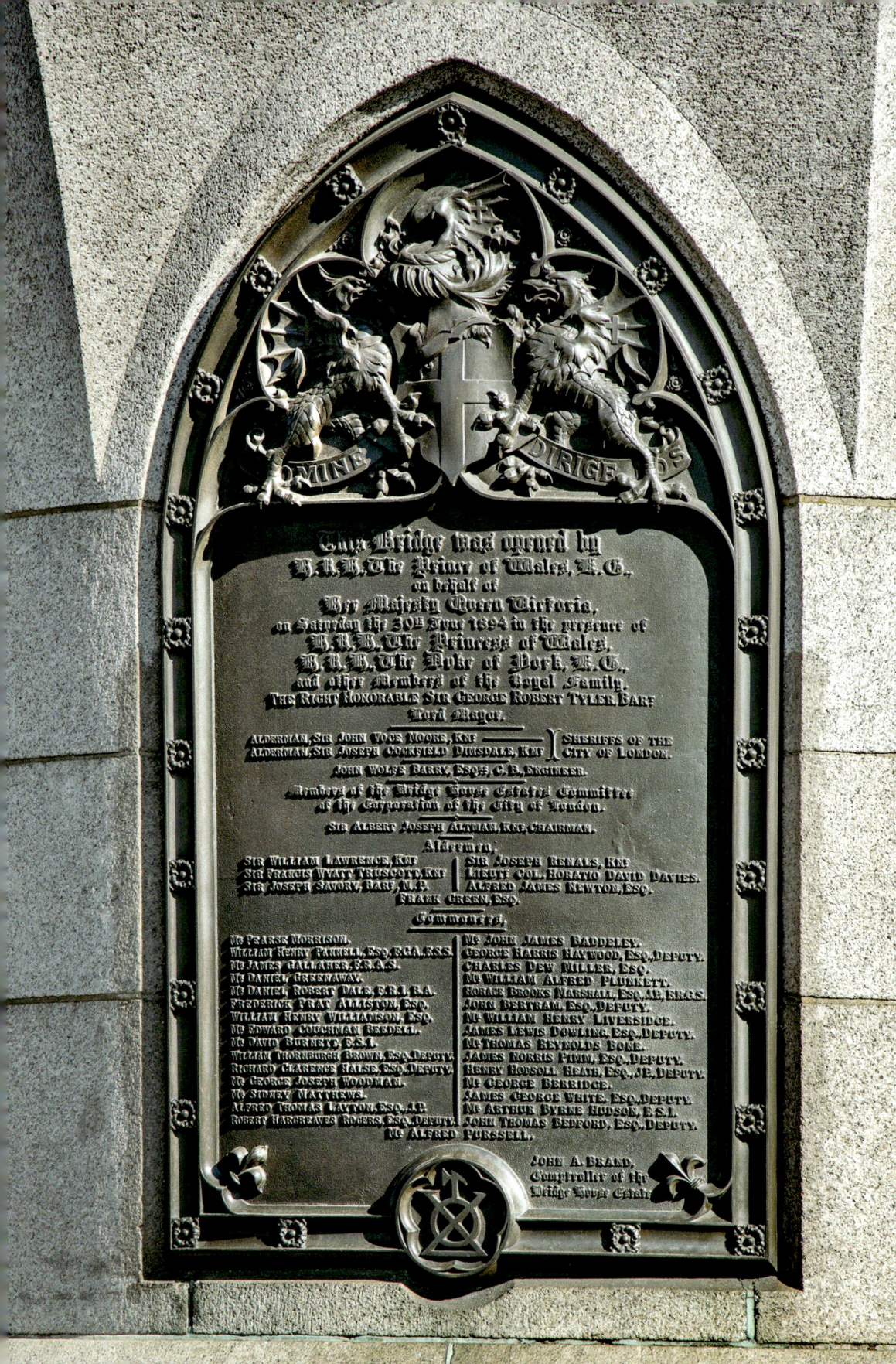

This Bridge was opened by
H.R.H. The Prince of Wales, K.G.,
on behalf of
Her Majesty Queen Victoria,
on Saturday the 30th June 1894 in the presence of
H.R.H. The Princess of Wales,
H.R.H. The Duke of York, K.G.,
and other Members of the Royal Family.
The Right Honorable Sir GEORGE ROBERT TYLER, Bart.
Lord Mayor.

ALDERMAN, SIR JOHN VOCE MOORE, Knt. ⎱ SHERIFFS OF THE
ALDERMAN, SIR JOSEPH COCKFIELD DIMSDALE, Knt. ⎰ CITY OF LONDON.

JOHN WOLFE BARRY, Esq., C.B., Engineer.

Members of the Bridge House Estates Committee
of the Corporation of the City of London.

SIR ALBERT JOSEPH ALTMAN, Knt., CHAIRMAN.

Aldermen.

SIR WILLIAM LAWRENCE, Knt.   SIR JOSEPH RENALS, Knt.
SIR FRANCIS WYATT TRUSCOTT, Knt. LIEUT. COL. HORATIO DAVID DAVIES.
SIR JOSEPH SAVORY, Bart., M.P.   ALFRED JAMES NEWTON, ESQ.
                 FRANK GREEN, ESQ.

Commoners.

Mr. PEARSE MORRISON.   Mr. JOHN JAMES BADDELEY.
WILLIAM HENRY PANNELL, ESQ., F.C.A., F.S.S.   GEORGE HARRIS HAYWOOD, ESQ., DEPUTY.
Mr. JAMES GALLAHER, F.R.A.S.   CHARLES DEW MILLER, ESQ.
Mr. DANIEL GREENAWAY.   Mr. WILLIAM ALFRED PLUNKETT.
Mr. DANIEL ROBERT DALE, F.R.I.B.A.   HORACE BROOKS MARSHALL, ESQ., M.A., F.R.G.S.
FREDERICK PRAT ALLISTON, ESQ.   JOHN BERTRAM, ESQ., DEPUTY.
WILLIAM HENRY WILLIAMSON, ESQ.   Mr. WILLIAM HENRY LIVERSIDGE.
Mr. EDWARD COUCHMAN BEEDELL.   JAMES LEWIS DOWLING, ESQ., DEPUTY.
Mr. DAVID BURNETT, F.S.I.   Mr. THOMAS REYNOLDS BONE.
WILLIAM THORNBURGH BROWN, ESQ., DEPUTY.   JAMES NORRIS PINN, ESQ., DEPUTY.
RICHARD CLARENCE HALSE, ESQ., DEPUTY.   HENRY HODSOLL HEATH, ESQ., J.P., DEPUTY.
Mr. GEORGE JOSEPH WOODMAN.   Mr. GEORGE BERRIDGE.
Mr. SIDNEY MATTHEWS.   JAMES GEORGE WHITE, ESQ., DEPUTY.
ALFRED THOMAS LAYTON, ESQ., J.P. Mr. ARTHUR BYRNE HUDSON, F.S.I.
ROBERT HARGREAVES ROGERS, ESQ., DEPUTY.   JOHN THOMAS BEDFORD, ESQ., DEPUTY.
              Mr. ALFRED PURSSELL.

JOHN A. BRAND,
Comptroller of the
Bridge House Estates.

INTRODUCTION

The manufacture of cast-metal signs is an aspect of Britain's industrial history about which remarkably little research has been carried out, and yet the output of the unsung but highly-skilled craftsmen who created those signs was essential, informative, instructive and undoubtedly saved countless lives. The sign-makers made everything from the little brass 'Do not use the toilet while the train is standing in the station' signs in railway carriages, and the nameplates and maker's plates on locomotives, right up to very large two-part signs – such as the one commemorating the opening of London's Tower Bridge, *left*, and the massive cast-iron instruction set on the back of the Great Western Railway's Swindon-built travelling crane (*see page 86*). Large signs like those two are hard to miss, but many of the smaller signs are easily overlooked – but once you start looking, they are everywhere.

opposite page: The plaque which commemorates the opening London's Tower Bridge by the Prince of Wales (later King Edward VII) in 1894 is a masterpiece of the pattern-maker and foundryman's skills. While the quality of the casting is remarkable, the work which must have gone into assembling the complex master pattern from which the mould was made must have been considerable.

left: Hotchkiss Circulators in the engine house at London's Tower Bridge, manufactured by Arthur Ross, Hotchkiss & Co. Ltd. of Glengall Road in Bermondsey, London. These devices collected and removed mud, air and oil from inside the steam boilers which drove the 1894-built Armstrong, Mitchell & Co. engines. The plaques were cast with a rectangular space into which the separately-cast 'discharge' plate was inserted while the plaque was still hot. As it cooled, it contracted and held the insert tightly in place.

right & above: The Devizes and Roundway War Memorial adjacent to St. John's Church in Devizes, Wiltshire, was designed by Francis William Troup, and erected in 1920-21. Six bronze panels, cast by Humphrys & Oakes at their Foundry in Fishponds, Bristol, honour the dead from World War I. Six smaller panels honour the dead from World War II. The panel, above, is the right-hand one It. Foundries across the country were involved in such work in the 1920s.

middle: Detail and maker's plate from a Class E Drop Valve Single Cylinder Engine, built in 1904 by Robey & Company at their Perseverance Works in Lincoln. It is now in the collection of the Robey Trust in Tavistock, Devon.

bottom: A cast-iron street sign now in the collection of the Fakenham Gasworks Museum in Norfolk.

INTRODUCTION

far left: The remains of the casting houses at Blaenavon Ironworks in South Wales. What makes Blaenafon especially interesting is an accident of its location and design. The site, while appearing on first sight to be very large is in fact very compact – a feature dictated by its geography – and it is that compactness which was its eventual downfall. As demand for iron grew, there was no opportunity for expansion, so the owners simply build a new complex at Forgeside on the other side of the valley near the Big Pit, leaving Blaenafon to the ravages of time, nature, and a growing local demand for dressed stone. Effectively abandoned by the end of the 19th century, the site did not undergo any of the successive modernisations which were necessary at other larger complexes. It was simply forgotten about, leaving it today as the most original and complete example of an 18th and 19th century ironworks in Britain.

above right: In the abandoned casting house at Blaenavon stands a 'New Star Mangle' – used in Victorian and Edwardian homes to wring water out of wet clothes – part of a range of high quality cast-iron domestic goods, manufactured by Smith & Paget of the Crown Works in Keighley, Yorkshire. Dating from 1890-1910, it is a good example of the intricate castings which were incorporated into even the most humble of domestic products at the time. Their best-selling mangle was the 'Crown', examples of which were exported all over the world.

The required range of skills which had to be brought together in the creation of these signs was considerable and included everything from typesetting skills more usually found in the printing industry through to the whole range of skills found in ironworks and foundries.

So, when did cast-iron signage first appear? Well opinions differ by several centuries. Several sources date it to the 1870s, when the 'Metallic Label Works' in Stratford-upon-Avon – later becoming known as the Royal Label Factory – started producing small cast iron plant labels much favoured by Queen Victoria for her royal gardens. That may be the first 'official' operation, but foundries across the country were certainly casting both lead and cast-iron signage more than 250 years before that – with cast brass already being used long before the end of the 18th century.

In the 19th century alone, millions must have been cast for a vast range of purposes but yet very little is known about the people who made them.

In most cases, the patterns from which they were made, and the moulds in which they were cast, had no lasting value, so almost all of them were disposed of after use, leaving few clues. This book explore the richness of the cast metal signs which survive, and hopefully gives a sense of the scale of their production.

But the value of the signage itself is immeasurable. Survivng signs offer us a succession of windows on history, helping today's historians unravel the often-complex legacies of the great companies which helped develop modern Britain.

Some great construction works, and industrial installations, were the result of the design and manufacturing skills of several companies so, once the promotional and advertising value of the cast-metal sign had been recognised, it was not uncommon for each participating company to want its plates to be visible to anyone admiring the machine in question.

Just such a collaboration was behind the building of – and later modifications and repairs to – the first mechanical paper-making machine at Frogmore Paper Mill in Hertfordshire, initially designed by two London stationers, the brothers Henry and Sealy Fourdrinier. The brothers' names thus became synonymous with these great machines, including the one – sadly now redundant – which still stands in the mill today.

above: The maker's plate as advertising – every Heidelberg platen 'letterpress' printing press had the maker's plate positioned at eye level and could not be ignored. Prototyped in 1914, these superbly well built and highly reliable machines were used all over the world and remained in production from 1923 until 1985.

above right: A specially-cast plaque celebrating the Heidelberg company's centenary in 1950.

right: An early 19th century cast-iron sign, on the wall of the 17th century Ye Olde King's Head pub and restaurant. The half-timbered building stands on the corner of Lower Bridge Street and Castle Street in Chester. (*image: Paul Fox*)

The design was based on an invention by Frenchman Louis-Nicholas Robert – modified by eminent Northumbrian-born engineer Bryan Donkin who was based in Bermondsey, London – and the first successful machine was installed in Frogmore in 1803 or 1804. It subsequently became known as the Fourdrinier Machine. The example currently at Frogmore was built in 1895 by James Bertram & Sons of Leith Walk in Edinburgh and includes parts by James Milne & Son of Milton House Works, Edinburgh, Ashworth & Parker of Bury, and Black Clawson of Newport in South Wales. How much of the original machine survives has not been determined, but the cast-metal plaques affixed to it all help tell its fascinating story.

Without them, no one would know that engineers and foundrymen from Scotland, England and Wales had all played key roles in the machine's 130-year history. That is the enduring fascination of the research which underpins this book.

Over the course of my researches, I have, as always, drawn very heavily on the knowledge and experience of a great many others, and to them all, I owe a debt of gratitude.

John Hannavy, Great Cheverell 2025

above: The author, *right*, and the late John Renwick who sponsored the plaque, at the unveiling in March 2004 of a cast metal 'blue plaque' marking the 185th anniversary of the birth in 1819 of the eminent Victorian photographer Roger Fenton. The author's biography of Fenton had been published 30 years earlier, in 1974.

below left: The large 1895 Fourdrinier Machine at Frogmore awaits restoration

below: The black Clawson maker's plate on one of the machine's drums.

bottom left: The replacement steam engine installed in 1956 was a 130hp inverted vertical two-cylinder duplex fully enclosed engine by Ashworth & Parker.

bottom right: James Milne and Son's maker's plate.

A LITTLE HISTORY

Almost five centuries separate objects in the two photographs below and opposite, but the technology use to create them is actually remarkably similar

Most histories start in the distant past and move forwards in time, but this one starts relatively recently, with a huge millennium project supported by the National Lottery. The scheme was designed to encourage cycling with the erection of cast-iron mileposts across the National Cycle Network. The essential casting techniques used to make those signs are centuries old.

In total, more than 1,000 of these iron structures were cast and installed from Lands End to Shetland in time for the start of the current century. They were cast by by Taylors Foundry of Haverhill, Suffolk. Twenty-five years on, a major refurbishment programme is already underway to restore some of these fascinating mileposts.

Four different designs were used in their creation – each by an artist/sculptor from one of the four nations which make up the United Kingdom – and the English version is based on a fossilised *Sigillaria* an extinct tree-like plant dating from 270 million years ago. It was created by sculptor John Mills and, in addition to simple directions, includes impressions of assorted fossils together with coded puzzles.

Cast-iron itself can trace its history back more than 4,000 years, probably to ancient China and Mesopotamia, where it was used for a wide range of applications such as making plough shares and weapons but in Europe there is little

opposite page: Brighton-based sculptor John Mills created the 'Fossil Tree' way-marker used on the National Cycle Network across England. This one is in Castlefields Park on Route 4 in Calne, Wiltshire. The three other designs are the work of Andrew Rowe from Swansea, Iain McColl from Glencoe and Belfast artist David Dudgeon.

below: Henry VIII''s royal insignia on one of the cast bronze cannon from the ill-fated *Mary Rose*, now displayed in the Mary Rose Museum at Portsmouth Historic Dockyard. These guns were cast between 1536 and 1540. While bronze-casting was already well established, iron-casting of large guns was still in its infancy. A quarter of a century later, most guns would be cast-iron. The largest surviving bronze guns from *Mary Rose* each weigh 2.7 tons.

below: The art of the sign-painter is kept alive in pub signs, still painted today as they have been for centuries. This photograph was taken at Wadworth's Brewery in Devizes, which still has a traditional sign-painting studio.

evidence of it being widely used before the 15th century. Then, hardly surprisingly, it was initially used for making cannonballs and other military artifacts.

Cast-metal signage, however, is a lot more recent. Men have been making signs, to guide, to inform or to warn, for millennia, but as long as the majority of the population could neither read nor write, that signage would by necessity have been non-verbal.

While places like hotels, inns and ale-houses all had names, they were usually represented in their signage primarily by pictograms – The Crown, The King's Head, The Swan and so on. The tradition of hand-painted pictographic pub signs continues to this day.

Despite an illiterate population, what we would recognise today as mileposts can be traced back to the development of the road network by the ancient Romans. Indeed, the term 'milepost' is a corruption of the Roman word 'mille' meaning one thousand. They introduced stone markers every 'mille' paces, incised with simple instructions or information. Today we would consider a Roman 'pace' to be two steps, and 1,000 of those double steps is actually about a mile.

In mediaeval times, there were relatively few signs – understandable with an ill-educated and widely illiterate population who rarely travelled further than a day's walking distance from their homes – and those who did, such as the drivers of mail and passenger coaches, knew their routes and rarely, if ever, deviated from them.

In Britain, the introduction of milestones and other way-markers came largely a result of the establishment of turnpike roads in the late 17th century – privately-maintained toll roads sanctioned by Acts of Parliament. These roads greatly improved travel conditions and, as a result, encouraged an increase in the movement of people and goods across the country. Knowing how far it was to London or Bristol became matters of greater significance than ever before – impacting both on journey time and cost.

When metal started to be used for signage, one of its early applications was probably for the creation of 'fire marks'. In the 17th and 18th centuries, before municipal fire services came along, putting fires out was a competitive business, with rival companies racing to the scene – and there were stories, almost certainly apocryphal, that if they got there and found that

far left: Used as one of the illustrations in Fothergill's *British Fire Marks from 1680*, this early cast lead mark was introduced by the 'New Bristol Fire Office' in the 1660s.

left: This Sun Fire Office mark, in cast lead c.1799, survives on a property in West Lavington, Wiltshire. The policy number, 566479, was hand-stamped into the sign.

below far left: A 'Phoenix Protection' fire plate from the late 18th century. The policy number is displayed beneath the phoenix emblem. Originally, a spearhead would have topped the diagonal spear, but that has been lost. This example, in cast lead, was used in the 1780s by the Phoenix Assurance Company.

left: A Norwich Union Fire Insurance Society plate, incorporating the logo of the former Hand in Hand Fire & Life Insurance Society. Early examples of this design were cast in lead, but this one is cast-iron. The Hand in Hand Fire Office, had been set up in 1696, later merging with Norwich Union which had been established a year later, the merged company adopting the former's 'hand-in-hand' logo.

the building was protected by a fire insurance company with which they were not in partnership, the firemen just watched the building burn. Much more likely was that they put the fire out and then sought compensation from the other insurance company. After all, with wooden-framed buildings, often with thatched roofs, letting the building next door continue to burn would have been fraught with risks of the fires spreading.

Insurance companies started issuing metal 'fire marks' to identify which properties had bought insurance with them, and such plates were affixed prominently to the fronts of buildings.

The first such plaques were either stamped out of sheets of lead, or cast in lead – a short-sighted idea, perhaps, as the temperature of a burning timber-framed house would significantly exceed the melting point of that lead sign – house fires burn at around 600°C while lead melts at a mere 327.5°C. These markers, represent one of the earliest applications of cast metal signage, with a date of between 1680 and 1683 being cited for the earliest surviving examples. Only grave markers date back further.

right: Six of the eight cast-iron grave slabs at the east end of St. George's Church in Burrington, Herefordshire. Furthest from the camera is the slab for Robert Steward, *see below*. The two largest slabs, measuring over three feet wide and nearly seven feet long, commemorate the lives of William Walker and Jane Hare, both of whom died in 1676, while the smaller slab to their left marks the passing of Maria Hare, presumably their daughter, just two years earlier. These grave slabs were originally located inside the church, but were relocated outside the east end in 1864 when the church was remodelled.

below: 'HERE LIETH THE BODY OF MARIA HARE WHO DECEASED THE FIRST DAY OF JUNE ANO (sic) DOM 1674'.

below right: The casat-iron grave slab memorialising Robert Steward, the inscription reading 'HERE LIETH ROBERT STEWARD WHO DECEASED THE 17 OF JANUARY 1619'. It is the oldest of the slabs.

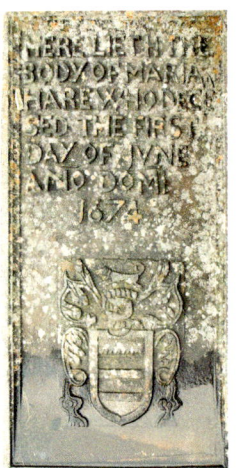

Many insurance companies had moved to cast-iron by the early years of the 19th century. Fire marks in copper, and later steel, were also widely used. The melting point of copper is 1,085 °C and steel is in the range of 1,205-1,370°C, so easily able to survive even the most ferocious of fires.

By the early years of the 20th century, seeking out and collecting fire marks had become something of a craze. In 1911, the first ever book on their history – *British Fire Marks from 1680* by George A. Fothergill – was published, and *The Antiquary*, a monthly magazine 'devoted to the past' published an article on the growing collecting craze, which included a brief history of fire services, and repeated the story of the alleged rogue behaviour of fire brigades past. Today, several hundred different fire marks are known to have been issued.

left: Three cast-iron grave marker plaques ready to be bolted to posts.

below: An iron marker and post cast as a single unit.

below left: When a plot was sold, a 'reserved' marker would usually replace the numbered one.

More than half a century before insurance plates started to appear – some just small cast plates, others full-size iron imitations of traditional ledger gravestones. About one hundred of these large cast-sheet memorials – usually referred to as 'ledger slabs' – are known to survive, mainly in the Weald area of Kent, but eight can also be seen in the graveyard of the church in the village of Burrington in the north of Herefordshire. These are believed to have been cast at nearby Bringewood Ironworks which could trace its history back to around 1585 in the reign of Queen Elizabeth I, but hardly a trace of it remains today.

The oldest of the Burrington grave slabs records the death of Robert Steward in January 1619, making clear that the inclusion of complex text content in the casting shed was already a well-developed skill. The dates of the deaths of those commemorated on the slabs range from 1619 to 1754.

The typography used on them includes both 'serif' and 'sans-serif' lettering, long before such typefaces were being introduced into the printing industry. One slab, commemorating Joyce Walker, and dated 1654, uses plain, or 'sans serif', lettering, while Richard Knight's slab from 1754 uses stylised 'Roman' or 'serif' lettering. 'Sans serif' had been in regular use by masons since at least the 12th century, but it was not until William Caslon designed his eponymous type-face in 1816 that the style was introduced to the printing industry and quickly adopted across the world.

above: Abraham Darby's elegant and pioneering Iron Bridge across the River Severn in Coalbrookdale, seen here shortly after its recent major restoration.

right: Thomas Telford's cast-iron Waterloo Bridge across the Afon Conwy at Betwys y Coed with its individually-cast letters.

Numbered grave markers can be traced back to the establishment of public cemeteries in the early years of the 19th century. It became a widespread practice for families to buy a plot in advance of the inevitable – after which some cemeteries would replace the numbered plaque with a 'Reserved' or 'Res' notice, also in cast-iron. Some manufacturers included their names in the moulds for these number posts, identifying them as having been produced by foundries local to the graveyards in which they were used. Thus, for example, we know that Stanford & Company of Colchester were still casting such gravemarkers right up until the outbreak of the First World War.

above: The Williamson Bros. of Kendal maker's plate on the 1879 Gayle Mill double vortex turbine. Williamson Brothers eventually became part of Gilbert Gilkes & Gordon.

left: The Thomson Double Vortex Turbine, manufactured by Williamson Bros. in 1879, is still in situ in Gayle Mill, Hawes, Yorkshire.

(both images courtesy of Gayle Mill)

In the old cemetery in Long Melford, Suffolk, is the largest collection of Victorian and Edwardian cast-iron 'gravestones' in Europe – more than 150 of them. They were made by the local foundry, Ward and Silver at their foundry in Hall Street.

Haden's of Market Place, Warminster in Wiltshire was another Victorian manufacturer, examples of whose cast-iron grave crosses, complete with their own name on the reverse – have been identified as far afield as New Zealand.

Abraham Darby III built the world's first iron bridge across the River Severn in Shropshire. The bridge proudly proclaims across the central span that 'This bridge was cast in Coalbrook-Dale and erected in the year MDCCLXXIX' – but, perhaps surprisingly, the lettering is painted on rather than cast into the metalwork. However, by the time master iron-founder William Hazledine, at his Plas Kyneston foundry, cast the ironwork for Thomas Telford's Waterloo Bridge at Betwys y Coed in 1815, each individual letter of the legend across the arch – 'THIS ARCH WAS CONSTRUCTED IN THE SAME YEAR THE BATTLE OF WATERLOO WAS FOUGHT' – was hand cast. The bridge, part of Telford's improved Holyhead Road, was opened to traffic the following year.

It is important to place the development of cast-metal signage within the context of Victorian industrial evolution. As has already been demonstrated, the incorporation of lettering into cast-iron objects had already been part of the foundryman's skill for at least two centuries – so below: The maker's name and lifting weight limit, cast into the upper balance block on an 1864-built Stothert & Pitt hand-cranked crane. Each of the balance blocks weighs 3 tons. The crane was recently restored by a team of volunteers – including former employees of the Bath-based crane-makers, and is now displayed on the site of the company's former Newark Works on Bath's riverside. One of the original buildings can be seen beyond the crane. While, initially, the company produced relatively small hand-operated cranes, they very quickly moved into much larger ones. By 1868, under licence from William Fairbairn who had patented its revolutionary design, they produced the large steam-operated swivel crane which still stands on Bristol's harbourside, and now restored, is occasionally steamed and put through its paces (see page 80). That crane's pioneering design enabled up to 35 tons of goods to be lifted directly from a ship's hold to waiting railway waggons and vice versa, greatly speeding up loading and unloading of cargo at Prince's Wharf in Bristol's renowned 'floating harbour'.

the creation of wooden hand-cut letters used in making the sand moulds was already an established craft, and there were plenty of those skilled craftsmen already employed in that industry. Those skills were essential in the creation of the master patterns from which the moulds for large metal signs were created.

The printing industry had long been using cast lead letters – introduced by Johannes Guttenberg in the mid-15th century – without which printed books like this volume could not have evolved.

During the massive expansion of British industry and manufacture in the 19th century, with huge mill engines being installed the length and

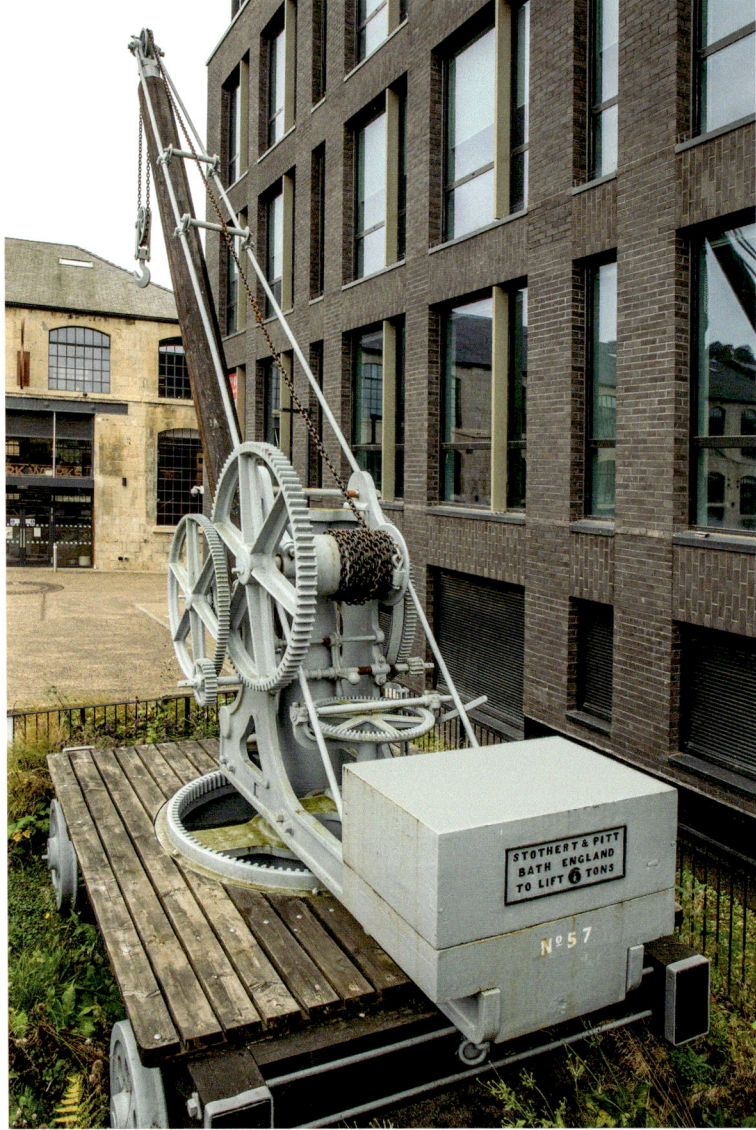

above left: Cast metal signage found uses everywhere. The 'turn' sign on the stop tap in the bath-house at the 'Big Pit' in South Wales advertises that the tap was made in 1939 by Bell & Smart of Tottenham Street in London.

above: 0-4-0ST Locomotive *Nora No.5* was built in 1920 by Andrew Barclay of Kilmarnock, Works No 1680, for the Blaenavon Colliery Co. Ltd.

left: A 'bare metal" plaque on the site of his Dartmouth workshop recalls Thomas Newcomen's first successful 'atmospheric' steam engine.

breadth of the country, cast-iron nameplates and makers' plates evolved as a simple, yet effective, form of industrial branding.

By the early years of the 20th century, just as on the railways, companies building those huge mill engines gave their machines names, with cast and polished brass plates identifying them.

below: Earnshaw and Holt of Canal Side Boiler and Engineering Works in Rochdale, were already established in business by 1864, when they supplied the 250hp engine (now preserved in Manchester's Science & Industry Museum) to A. and J. Law's Durn Mill in Littleborough, By 1864 the partnership of Thomas Stephen Holt and Edward Earnshaw had been dissolved.

A fine example of this practice is the massive 2,500hp four-cylinder triple expansion steam engine which once powered Trencherfield Mill in Wigan – a large spinning mill by the side of the Leeds & Liverpool Canal. To all intents and purposes, this behemoth is two engines side-by-side, so it has two names – *Helen* and *Rina* after the wives of the mill's directors.

Cast-iron and cast-brass were the two most commonly-used materials and, on engines, many such plates were finished, polished and painted or enamelled to a very high standard – reflecting the manufacturers' intentions that these plates should reflect the build-quality of their machines and enhance their reputations.

The builders of those huge mill engines clearly saw the merits of such advertising. The recognition that a simple cast plaque could both enhance sales and promote a business created a huge demand.

On the railways, even a humble coal wagon would have two individually cast plates identifying the vehicle itself – the heavy-duty equivalent of car numberplates today. The huge numbers of such signs and plates which proliferated on the railways are discussed later in this book.

When steam-powered road engines began to appear on the scene, they too were given names, generating a lot more work for the skilled foundrymen who created makers' plates and numberplates in their tens of thousands.

Over the years as steam engines moved on to the fairground, the typography used on

above: The giant engine at Trencherfield Mill in Wigan was built by J. & E. Wood at their Victoria Foundry in Bolton in 1907.

right: Steam is introduced into the Trencherfield engine via *Rina*, the high-pressure cylinder, then under the engine-house floor to *Helen*, before being split into feeds for the two low pressure cylinders. Rina and Helen each have a beautifully cast brass and enamel nameplate.

their signage became more sophisticated. Showmen's engines with their ornate metalwork, kept highly polished to sparkle under the profusion of fairground lights, had nameplates and maker's plates to match. Highly detailed brass castings were created for these machine

Amongst the leaders in this market were Savages of King's Lynn in Norfolk, whose engines epitomised the glamour of the Victorian and Edwardian fairground. Frederick Savage himself is credited with the development of the centre-mounted horizontal steam engine which powered merry-go-rounds which the company exported all over the world. As the engine was in full view right in the middle of the ride, it needed to be built to the very highest standard of finish, and thus it moved from simply being a functioning piece of equipment to being a lavish statement of quality, sparkling under the lights and becoming a fitting addition to the magical world of the fairground.

above left: This cast plate attests to the huge number of engines which the company must have been built.

above: The maker's plate from a Wallis & Steevens steam roller.

below left: The maker's plate on a steam engine at Bursledon brickworks

below: The maker's plate on a steam-driven pug mill at Bursledon brickworks. S. S. Stott & Co of Laneside Foundry, Haslingden, built a range of stationary engines.

left: This Savages engine, *Ladygolightly*, was built in 1896 and, with Works No.664, sports several cast- and pressed-metal name and number plates. The difference in typographic style used for the nameplates on this engine, and *John Bull*, below, raises the possibility that the buyers may have been offered some say in the typeface and style used, either by Savages of King's Lynn or by the builders of the fairground rides they powered.

middle: The centre engine John Bull was built by Savages in 1895, carrying works number 638.

bottom: Down's Gallopers at the erstwhile Great Dorset Steam Fair a few years ago. The ride is powered by Savage engine *John Bull*.

opposite page: The cast brass maker's plate on a 1902 Merryweather 'Greenwich Gem' fire engine. Now on display in the fire museum at Highlands End Holiday Park in Eype, Dorset, the engine is on permanent loan from Bridport Museum. The pumps on Merryweather Gem fire appliances, were driven by a twin-cylinder, vertical boiler, steam engine.

top: Galloway's of Manchester's placed their maker's name on cast brass bands around the front of the Lancashire boilers which powered the machinery at Coldharbour Mill, a woollen spinning and weaving mill in Devon.

middle left: The cast brass maker's name on the furnace door on Cornish boiler which generated steam for the brine pump. at the Lion Salt Works in Northwich, Cheshire, was made in 1891 by little-known boiler-maker William Lord of Lord Street Iron Works in Bury, Lancashire. All we know of him derives from this door front.

middle: The maker's plate around the fire doors on Crofton Pumping Station's Lancashire boilers in Wiltshire, tell us they were built at the GWR Swindon Works.

middle right: On this boiler at Coldharbour Mill, Devon, J. & J. Neil & Co. of Glasgow cast their name into the furnace doors.

bottom: The now-redundant Lancashire Boilers in the engine house at what is now known as the Westonzoyland Pumping Station Museum of Steam Power and Land Drainage, was built in 1914 by Fred Danks Ltd of Oldbury, Birmingham.

Judging by the typographic variety which can be seen in the nameplates on surviving fairground centre engines, the craftsmen who made their highly finished plaques had a range of typefaces at their disposal, suggesting the possibility that customers – who presumably chose the names for their engines they were buying – might also have had a say in the final appearance of the nameplates themselves.

From a commercial point of view, that would be understandable – a measure of uniformity in the appearance of the maker's plate, for advertising and promotion, and a measure of individuality in the engine's nameplate to reflect customer individuality. But as none of that was written down anywhere, it is simply conjecture on the part of this particular writer.

While machine-builders and others clearly saw the potential commercial advantage of either using maker's plates or casting their names and other information into the machines themselves to promote their businesses, another popular reason for commissioning signage was really little more than corporate vanity, with councillors across the country seeking to see themselves immortalised in large plaques celebrating what they considered to be their enduring achievements, and their contributions to civic society.

On 14 December 1836, James Dredge, a Bath brewer-turned-civil-engineer, was granted British Patent No.7120, for an innovative re-imagining of the design for a suspension bridge and, lest anyone thought they might be free to replicate the design, he had cast-iron plates and pediments affixed to his bridges asserting his patent rights.

In seeking that patent, he did something that the 19th century's most celebrated bridge-builders, Thomas Telford and Isambard Kingdom

top left: Cast-iron plaque commemorating the tramway in Christchurch on New Zealand's South Island.

top: This W. & F. Wills engine, with its elaborate maker's plate gives us maker, date and patent number. It is preserved in the Westonzoyland Pumping Station Museum of Steam Power and Land Drainage

above: The maker's plate on a steam engine built by Galloways of Manchester and now preserved in the Science & Industry Museum, Manchester.

top: The commemorative plaque on the side of the LNER's record-breaking Gresley 'A4 Pacific', *Mallard*, on the occasion of it achieving the world-record speed for a steam locomotive of 126 miles per hour – a record which still stands today, and which will now never be broken due to the speed restrictions placed on steam locomotives.

above middle: built by Cope, Sherwin & Company of Shoreditch, London, in 1828, the Imperial Press was considered one of the finest platen presses of its day. Built out of cast-iron, it was in production for only a few years. However, quite a number can still be found being used in art schools and in the studios of fine-art printmakers. Their high-quality castings and simple mechanisms made them reliable workhorses.

bottom: Traditionally, the starting point for paper-making involved the shredding and recycling of cotton rags. This rag-shredder is preserved in the former paper mill at Wookey Hole in Somerset, its cast-iron water bath carrying the name of its maker – Thomas J. Marshall of Bishopsgate in London. It was installed in the mill in 1848. Marshall exhibited a range of paper-making machines at the 1862 International Exhibition. Wookey Hole paper mill was renowned for the quality of the papers it produced, some of which was used to print banknotes.

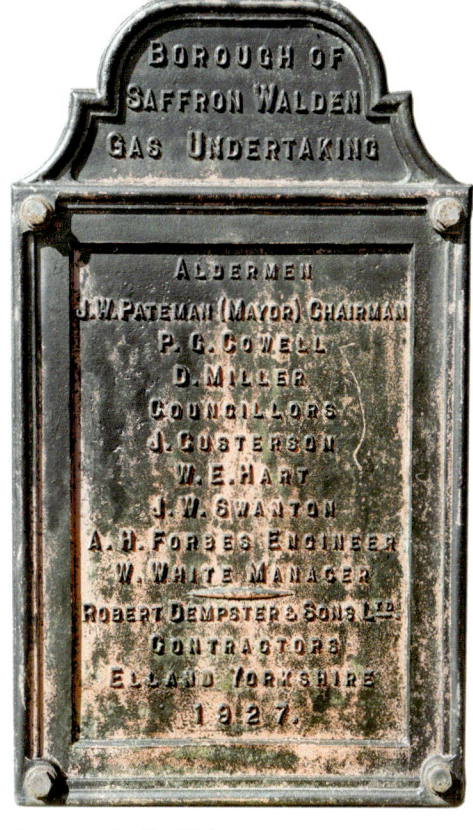

Brunel, had never felt the need to do – he took out a patent for those aspects of his design which he considered original. His design incorporated elements of the traditional suspension bridge, married to what we might recognise today as elements of a cable-stayed structure. He called his design a 'Taper Suspension Bridge', and it worked on the principle of a double cantilever structure. Central to his patent was the use of wrought iron rods rather than chain or cables, angled in towards the carriageway, rather than being hung vertically. This design, he asserted, improved the stability of the bridge, and in fact it was

above left: One of the many surviving artifacts at Fakenham Gasworks Museum in Norfolk. The Engineer and Manager had to be named.

above: Also preserved at Fakenham, the civic dignitaries involved in the establishment of Saffron Walken's 'Gas Undertaking' are all memorialised in cast-iron.

left: The 1981 plaque marking the 75th anniversary of the opening of the Newport Transporter Bridge in South Wales.

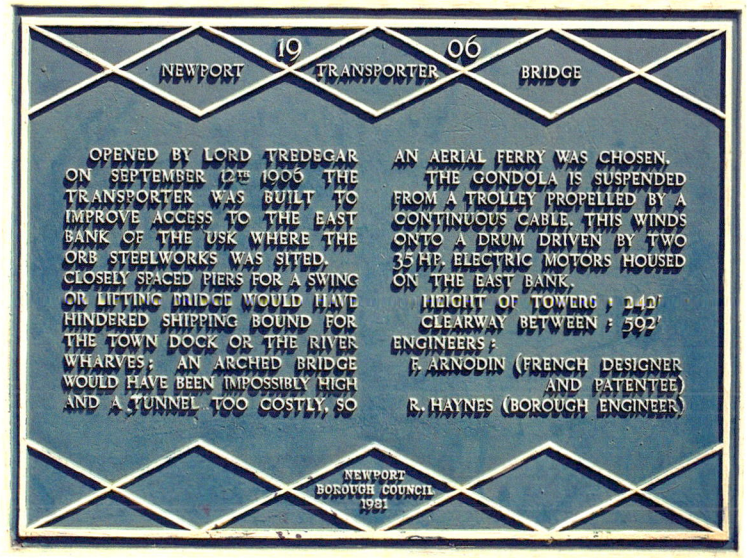

right: The patented angled chains on James Dredge's Victoria Bridge over the River Avon in Bath, opened in December 1836. This bridge opened in the same month he was granted patent protection. It is the oldest surviving bridge built to his patented design.

below: To remind people that he had the weight of the law on his side, Dredge included the Royal coat of arms on the plaque which was bolted to one of the bridge's towers. Whether or not he had the right to do so is unclear.

so stable that if someone had decided to cut the bridge in half across the centre, both halves of the structure could have remained suspended in place. The total weight of the carriageway and suspension bars reduced towards the centre, so the bulk of the bridge's load was carried by the towers or abutments.

He designed and built more than 50 bridges – several examples of his work survive. For the Wilcot bridge – built in 1845 as a private crossing over the Kennet and Avon Canal on the Stowell Park estate near Pewsey, Wiltshire – his assertion of his patent rights takes is cast into the iron

right: The shortest of the bridges designed by James Dredge still spans the Kennet & Avon Canal in Wilcot, Wiltshire, although it is now in very poor condition. It was commissioned by local landowner, Col. Wroughton, and completed in 1845. Here, Dredge used cast-iron columns rather than stone towers to support the cabling. The cast-iron pediments carry his patent claims.

pediments bridging the tubular cast-iron columns which form the towers at either side of the canal. So in that instance, they form part of the structural integrity of the bridge rather than simply as an advertisement.

Cast metal signage very quickly became ubiquitous, in use across every aspect of 19th and 20th century society, its clarity durability and repeatability making it ideal for all sorts of messaging in all sorts of situation.

When powered flight became possible, engine makers were quick to see the sales benefit of having their names emblazoned on their engines. In those early days, aircraft builders – many of them aviators themselves – sought the most powerful, the fastest, or the lightest engines to power their machines.

One way to draw attention to their potential was to promote their use in the many races and endurance flights which dominated the early years, with the public drawn to air shows across the contry. One of the earliest air shows took place over Blackpool in 1909, largely using French-designed Farman aircraft using French-built engines.

An early market leader was the Societé des Moteurs Gnome whose engines powered the French-built, multi-trophy-winning Farman aircraft flown by British aviator Claude Grahame-White and others. It would later power legendary British aircraft such as the Sopwith Pup.

The Farman, like many early aircraft – Blériot's was an exception – had the engine and propellor behind the pilot, and the engine had no cowling over its radial cylinders, its maker's plate thus highly visible.

above left: The 7-cylinder Gnome Omega radial engine was one of the more reliable early aircraft engines, and powered a number of British- and French-built aircraft. This early example is displayed at the RAF Museum at Cosford, Shropshire. Above it is superimposed the cast-brass maker's plate from the Gnome engine.

above: An early adopter of the Gnome engine was the Sopwith Company of Kingston upon Thames, who used in their Sopwith 1½ Strutter, and Pup aircraft.

right: The enamelled cast-metal maker's plate on Whitehead Governor No.937 affixed to the Pollitt & Wigzell steam engine, preserved in Birmingham's Thinktank Museum. The governor was invented and patented by Harold Whitehead, who described himself as a 'mechanical draughtsman'. He was an engineer with Scott & Hodgson of Manchester and claimed to have sold more than 500 of his patent spring-loaded governors in their first 10 years – between 1894 and 1904.

middle: The Pollitt & Wigzell engine's Whitehead Governor sits on top of the metal post in the middle left of the picture, its spinning metal balls used to control the speed of the engine – an early semi-automatic control system. As the engine speed increaed, centrifugal force made the balls spin outwards, thus applying a steam shut-off valve to bring speed back under control.

bottom: The grey cast-metal maker's plate on a Series 2 Field-Marshall diesel tractor built by Marshall, Sons & Company at their Britannia Works in Gainsborough, Lincolnshire. Marshall had pioneered the manufacture of diesel-engined tractors back in 1929. The company had just merged with John Fowler & Company of Leeds when this model was launched in 1948, briefly becoming part of the British Leyland group in the 1970. Tractor production ended in 1992.

left: This 6-stroke gas engine was built by Dick, Kerr & Company of Preston and Kilmarnock, under licence from Griffin & Co – who did not have the manufacturing capacity at their Bath works – and was supplied new to Beckton Gas Works. The 'Griffin's Patent' plate is nearest the left-hand end of the engine, with the Dick, Kerr & Company plate to the right.

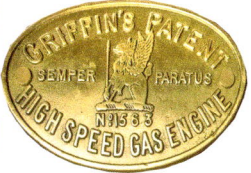

above: The Griffin company's nameplate on the 1882 engine built for Samuel Griffin by Dick, Kerr & Company.

As many of the spectators were potential aviators themselves, and 'health and safety' was not yet a consideration, they could gather round the successful planes and pilots.

The manufacture and use of cast-metal signs was so widespread that it is remarkable that, in the research carried out for this book, no instruction manuals for trainee pattern-makers and mould-makers – specifically addressing the challenges of creating the typography for such signs – has so far been located. The closest yet found is a reference to the patterns being made 'in the usual manner'. Given the Victorian enthusiasm for producing instruction books for just about everything, for a branch of industry with such wide applications, that has been quite a surprise.

We must assume that the absence of such material means that training was given entirely on the job. In the textile world, this was known in Victorian and Edwardian times as 'sitting next to Nellie', but in the almost-entirely male domain of the pattern shop and foundry, there must have been another name for it. That absence almost certainly means that there are gaps in the stories told on the pages which follow, but the scale on which such signage was produced is undeniable. Foundrymen must have found it challenging, at times, to keep up with demand for their skills.

There any more examples of their craftsmanship surviving than we might expect – but if we are not actively looking, we just don't notice them. Looking for original cast-metal signage today is a fascinating journey of discovery – it is only when we are actively looking for them that we notice examples we have walked past on many previous occasions.

below: Commemorative cast-iron trivets were produced in huge numbers as part of the merchandising to mark the late Queen Elizabeth's Silver Jubilee in 1977. They were produced at Park Foundry in Belper, Derbyshire, a division of the Parkray company, more famous for its range of cast-iron stoves.

right: A dis-used Victorian wall-mounted posting box, one of the earliest designs introduced in 1857 – just seven years after the first cylindrical pillar box had been installed on the island of Jersey. It was the first to be recessed into a wall. It was mainly used in locations where there was likely to be only light usage, or where there was insufficient space on the pavement for a conventional pillar box. It was cast in Birmingham by Smith and Hawkes at their Eagle Forge & Foundry Company. They cast at least three different design variants of this box, over a period of many years. This example is preserved at Great Malvern railway station. (*photo: Paul Fox*)

far right: Often referred to as a '24-hour Post Office' this combined telephone kiosk, post box and stamp machine – known officially as the K4 – was designed in 1924 but not installed anywhere until 1930. The simple 'GR' was the King's cipher. The two stamp machines usually sold 1d and ½d stamps – the cost of posting a letter had gone up from 1d in 1910 to 1½d in 1918. The K4 had a footprint half as big again as the standard K2 kiosk then currently in use and, despite its dual functionality, did not prove popular on the pavements of Britain. Only 50 were built, between 1930 and 1935, so they are now very rare. In damp and humid weather, the adhesive on the stamps caused them to stick together on the roll. This example is part of the National Collection of Telephone Kiosks at the Avoncroft Museum near Bromsgrove, while another is preserved at Amberley Museum in Sussex, and a third, installed in 1932, in Frodsham, Cheshire.

Take, for example, the ubiquitous postbox, produced by Royal Mail in a variety of shapes and sizes since shortly after Rowland Hill introduced the penny post in 1840, many of them reflecting the typographic styles of the period. Originally in cast-iron, and later in steel, examples survive from every monarch since Victoria. Each monarch had their own cipher cast into letter boxes installed during each reign, and there were even 200 cast during the short reign of King Edward VIII. Queen Victoria actually had two, and so did the late Queen Elizabeth – 'EIIR' on English and Welsh letter boxes, the Scottish crown north of the border – the Scots objected to the use of EIIR, quite rightly pointing out that she was the first Queen Elizabeth of Scotland, the 16th century queen having only reigned over England and Wales.

For the past three years, the cipher of King Charles III has appeared on new post boxes and, ironically, on the locomotives which haul the Royal Train – just a few months before the decision was made to cancel the train.

But that is the thing with signage – much of it is temporary and transient, and can go from being essential to being unnecessary at the stroke of a pen or as a result of the passage of time.

The two locomotives, numbered 67005 and 67006, which have been used for many years to pull the royal train formerly carried cast-metal

left: The Royal Cypher on Class 67 No.67005 *King's Messenger*, one of the two locomotives which haul the Royal Train.

far left: Maker's name cast into an agricultural oat crusher manufactured by Wallace (Glasgow) Ltd. The company was established in 1919, initially building the Burt-McCollum single sleeve valve petrol engine, the patent rights for which it had recently acquired. Those engines were used in Argyll cars, and early aircraft. The company had diversified into agricultural machinery by the late 1920s around which time it sold its patent rights in the engine to a car manufacturer in Detroit, Michigan, USA.

nameplates *Queen's Messenger a*nd *Royal Sovereign*. As if to underline the transient nature of signage, 67005 now carries the King's cipher, with new nameplates made carrying the name *King's Messenger*. Even those will retire into history when the royal train is withdrawn from service in 2027.

Today, tapping in to the nostalgia and retro markets, there is a huge market on websites such as ebay and etsy for replica cast-iron signs. There are also growing numbers of delightful spoofs, such as a brass sign claiming to be from 1868 on which 'His Grace the Duke of Gumby' announces that 'Poachers will be shot and, if practicable, questioned afterwards'. There never was any such Duke, despite many on-line sites claiming it is a genuine antique. 'Caveat emptor' is always good advice when buying online.

The nostalgia culture has also seen a rebirth in the use of cast metal for heritage signage, with traditional early 20th century fingerpost designs being re-introduced across the country. They may now be cast in aluminium or one of the many alloys and composites available, and cast or moulded from CNC-cut patterns, but they look the part. Nostalgia is, as they say, the thing of the future

below left: Parish boundary markers for the parishes of St. Peter le Poer, and St. Andrew's in Holborn, London. The annual ritual of 'Walking the bounds' is still observed in many places, with congregations processing around the parish boundaries and stopping at each marker. (photo: Eileen Gunn)

below right: These plates are for St Peter le Poer, again, and St Marylebone (photo: Eileen Gunn)

MAKING CAST-METAL SIGNS

The required range of talents which had to be brought together in the creation of cast metal signs was considerable and included everything from typesetting – more usually found in the printing industry – through to the whole range of highly specialised skills employed in ironworks and foundries.

Opinions as to when such signs started to appear differ by some centuries, with a number of sources even disregarding all the evidence before the 1870s, when the wonderfully-named 'Metallic Label Works' in Stratford-upon-Avon – later becoming known as the Royal Label Factory – started producing small cast iron plant labels much favoured by Queen Victoria for her royal gardens.

As mentioned in the previous chapter, foundries across the country were certainly casting lead and iron fire marks almost a century before that. Signage – initially wooden and then metal – proliferated in the late 17th and early 18th centuries as both literacy and transport improved. A typical 19th century example would be the 1814 plaque which is affixed to one of the mock-baronial towers of Thomas Telford's pioneering Craigellachie Bridge over the River Spey in Scotland.

opposite page: The 1814 cast iron signs on one of the towers of Thomas Telford's Craigellachie Bridge which spans the River Spey in the village of the same name in Moray. The upper sign was cast in two sections – causing uneven spacing of the letters at the join – by Telford's ironmaster of choice, William Hazledine, at his Plas Kynaston foundry in North Wales. The signs, along with the ornate lattice ironwork of the bridge itself, were transported by barge along the Ellesmere Canal to Ellesmere Port where they were transferred to ships to be sailed all the way round the North of Scotland to Speymouth. The last few miles being covered by horse and cart.

left: Telford's elegant Craigellachie Bridge from the riverbank. In 1814 the design and construction of the bridge were at the leading edge of technology, and shipping all the ironwork from Ruabon to the bridge site posed a considerable logistical challenge.

right: Sometimes, the challenges facing the man who typeset the lettering seem insignificant when compared with the delicate ornate castings surrounding the plaque. Now preserved in the Summerlee Museum of Scottish Industrial Life in Coatbridge, Ayrshire, this octagonal cast-iron Drinking Fountain and 'Pavilion' was made by Walter Macfarlane & Company of the Saracen Foundry, Glasgow. These fountains were produced in some number to celebrate Queen Victoria's Golden Jubilee in 1887, and this one formerly stood in Dunbeth Park, Coatbridge. The plaque carries the legend 'Presented to the Burgh of Coatbridge by the Building Trades 22nd June 1887'. A variant was also cast to mark the Queen's Diamond Jubilee in 1897.

below right: This sign, on White Mill (or Whitemill) Bridge over the River Stour near Sturminster Marshall, was erected after a law was passed in 1827, in the reign of King George IV. The eight-arch bridge to which it is affixed dates from the 16th century.

Despite the fact that his foundry was hundreds of miles away in North Wales, William Hazledine clearly saw the commercial potential of advertising his achievements to the passengers in every coach which trundled across the bridge.

Just a few years later, in 1828, a rather draconian sign was installed on Whitemill Bridge over the River Stour near Sturminster Marshall in Dorset. That particular sign was probably of little social value, as the majority of those who might be considered likely to deface the bridge would almost certainly have been unable to read the warning of dire consequences which it announced. It is interesting to note that, even at this early date,

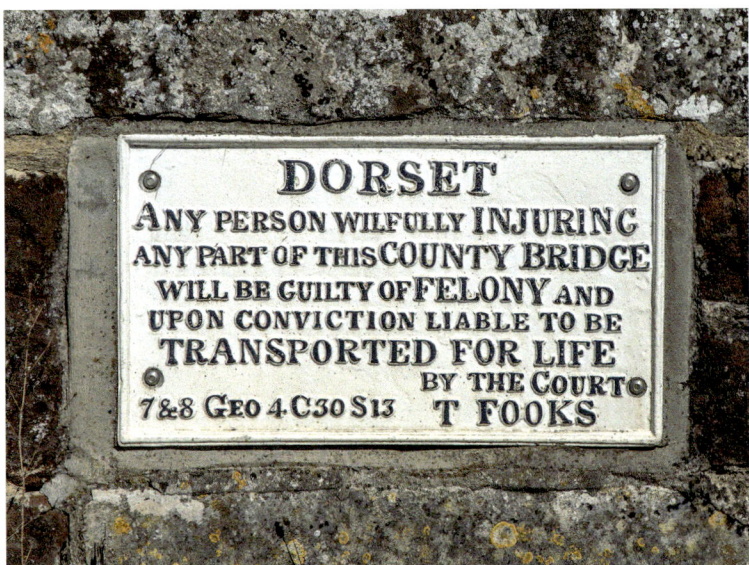

typographic style and size were already being used to emphasise, ownership of the bridge, potential crimes, and threatened punishment.

One of the key components in casting metal signs – apart from the metal itself, that is – is what is often referred to as 'green sand' although, perversely, not all 'green sand' is green in colour, the term now being more widely used to identify the sand's properties rather than its colour. It is highly compactable and retains moisture long enough to 'set' to a particular shape.

It is the sort of sand we would all have loved as children when building sandcastles on the beach – no collapsing walls or towers as the sun dried the castle out too quickly.

Green sand is a sedimentary layer from the Cretaceous Period, laid down between 145 million and 66 million years ago, and the mineral-rich variety on which this writer's house was built is actually a dark khaki-green colour. While predominantly silica, it contains both clay and chalk, as well as fine particles of iron ore and other minerals. Once dug out, it soon changes colour from green to brown as the iron particles oxidise. Once compacted, however, it is very firm indeed.

An essential constituent of the sand is clay, and the sand/clay mixture has the right characteristics for making a sand mould when a moist handful, tightly gripped, retains its shape perfectly when released. If it has dried out a little, the die-maker would simply add a bit more water until his experience told him the consistency was correct.

Once compacted, the sand can withstand a considerable amount of pressure without fracturing – so solid, in fact, that the oldest parts of the author's cottage had no need of foundations when built on a bed of it in the middle of the 18th century.

Once the idea of cast typographic signs was introduced, they proliferated, ranging in size from the relatively simple – like the White Mill Bridge sign *opposite* – to large and complex designs such as the elaborate cast bronze plaque erected on London's Tower Bridge to commemorate its opening (*see page 4*).

Despite their age and scale, the processes for making such plaques on were fundamentally the same. The only significant differences over the years have been how the individual letters were cut – for the Tower Bridge plaque each would have been hand cut, while for modern blue plaques a computer numerical control cutter (CNCC) is often used to make the master pattern.

above: The cast-iron maker's plate on a barring engine – used to start a large mill engine – c.1880s, by George Saxon of Openshaw, Manchester. Seen in the Science Museum store at Wroughton, Wiltshire.

below: A cast-metal bridge sign, showing weight limits, introduced after the 1903 Railway Act, now displayed in the Colonel Stephens Museum at Tenterden Station in East Sussex.

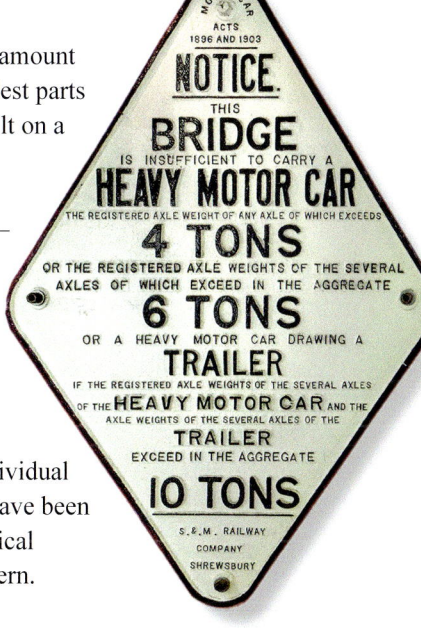

opposite page: The casting floor in the workshops of the former Dinorwig slate quarries, now the National Slate Museum of Wales. It sits at the heart of the Welsh slate landscape, recently designated a World Heritage Site. The workshop-men prided themselves that they could repair any and every piece of equipment used in the quarries and in the workshops themselves. Towards the bottom right of the picture is a sand mould still in its casting frame and, to its left, the iron casting made from it

top: Near the site of the house which he rented in Wigan whilst writing *The Road to Wigan Pier*, a plaque commemorates the life and work of George Orwell (Eric Blair).

below left: Known as a 'German Bench', this robust pattern-maker's workbench was illustrated in *The Pattern Maker's Handybook* by Paul N. Hasluck, published in 1887.

bottom: Also in Wigan, a 'blue plaque' recalls the birthplace of the town's other famous 'George' – the music-hall star George Formby Senior. who was the originator of the jokes about Wigan Pier.

Some of the sign-maker's essential skills were akin to those of the graphic designer and typographer – but with one very important difference.

In Victorian and Edwardian times, the bulk of the work in the printing industry used the letterpress process, where the letters were inked up and then brought into contact with the paper using a flatbed or platen printing press. That, of course, required the original wooden or metal letters to be made back-to-front so that the printed image would read the right way round. For cast metal sign-making, the letters had to be the right way round to start off with, so the craftsmen who made the wooden block letters would hand cut right-reading masters for making the moulds.

Several early writers lamented the paucity of practical instructions in the available manuals – even books specifically written for apprentices offered scant detail. Writing in the introduction, to his 1905 manual *Pattern Making and Foundry Practice,* L. H. Hand offered an unsatisfactory explanation, putting that down to the fact that when traditions are as old as metal casting, the skills and techniques must already be well established, noting that:

'Among the relics of prehistoric man there are weapons, implements and vessels of bronze which, by

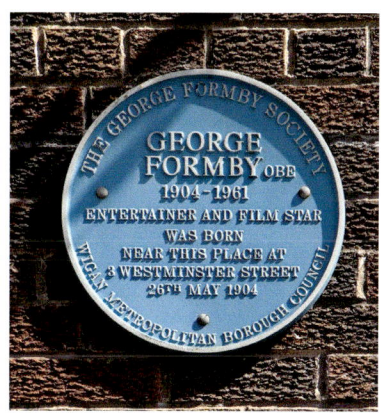

top: The hardwood pattern used to make the moulds for the Rhymney's 'K Class' locos Nos.100-105.

above: The GWR stock number on the reverse.

below: The pattern of pinholes forms a visual history of where the figures for the other numbers had been fixed.

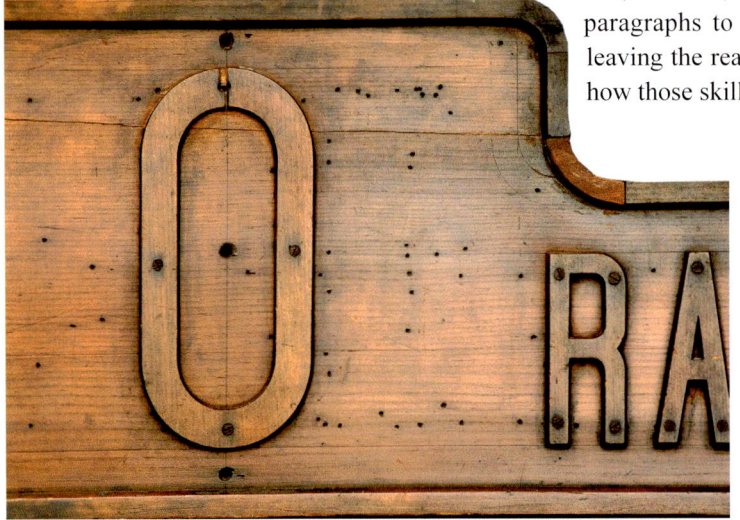

inevitable inference, we must concede were cast in moulds made by embedding either a pattern of wood or other material in sand or earth... ...Patient scientific research has revealed incontrovertible evidence that the art of moulding in earth is one of great antiquity, and this justifies the deduction that pattern making also as a craft, though no doubt struggling through long periods of time in a state of primitive crudity, is of almost equally remote origin...'

Having said all that, however, he limited his examples to heavy industrial casting, leaving the finer skills for making signage largely unexplored.

One of the very few manuals to give any hint as to the procedures for making cast-metal nameplates was *The Principles of Pattern Making written specially for apprentices and students in technical schools,* by Joseph G. Horner, published by Sir Isaac Pitman & Sons in 1903. Even there, however, the author devoted just two paragraphs to the subject, not actually leaving the reader any wiser at all about how those skills were acquired:

'The patterns of name plates are made in all sizes and forms, usually of wood. A thin piece of wood is planed and cut to the outline required, and filletting is glued or nailed around the edges. Lines are drawn upon the plate,

left: 'K Class' 0-6-2ST locomotive No.104, one of 48 built for the Rhymney Railway. The final batch, built by Neilson Reid & Co in Glasgow in 1900, were numbered 100 to 105. The master pattern for their numberplates is opposite. The plates are believed to have been cast at the Rhymney's workshops near Cardiff Docks, before such operations were transferred to new workshops in Caerphilly, in 1901.

and letters of lead or brass are cemented on with varnish, or are nailed on, or in the case of heavy patters, are screwed on.'

According to Joseph A. Shelley in his 1920 book *A Treatise on the Construction and Application of Patterns,* originally published in America, finely made sets of letters were readily available by that time:

'Pattern letters are used for reproducing firm names, identification letter, or figures on castings...They are made of either brass or a soft alloy of tin and lead, and they may be procured in three styles, known as "Roman," "sharp-faced Gothic," and "flat-faced Gothic." The sizes range in height from 1/8 inch to 4 inches. The brass pattern letters are used on metal patterns and the sort metal ones on wood, as they are easily bent to conform to curved surfaces.'

How those lead or brass letters themselves were cast is not explored, but presumably they were sourced from the same foundries which cast lead letters for the printing industry – except that they would be right-reading rather than reversed.

The required words would be assembled and pinned or pegged on to a board, following a pre-drawn template, creating the master from which the sand mould would be made. That wooden matrix or 'pattern' would be used until

below: Part numbers cast into the Walschaerts valve gear on a 1954 Brighton-built British Railways Class 4MT 2-6-4 tank engine. Invented by Belgian engineer Egide Walschaerts in the 1840s, it was the first design to be fitted outside the locomotive frames, simplifying servicing. The first British locomotive to be fitted with Walschaerts valve gear was a Swindon, Marlborough & Andover Railway Fairlie-designed 0-4-4T in 1878.

right: An assembled wooden pattern – hand-cut letters on a wooden base. It is clear from the condition of some of the letters that they have been used multiple times. (Image: Croft Castings Ltd.)

below: From a paper published in the *Journal of the American Foundrymen's Association* in October 1899, a useful table on the shrinkage characteristics of various metals

bottom left: GWR 'Banana Van' plate, cast as a single piece. Standardisation of wagon plate design was encouraged by the Railway Clearing House in the 1920s.

bottom right: Identification plate from a 1953-built 10-ton British Railways insulated van using interlocking wooden numbers, letters and spacers which fitted into slots on the master board.

it was so worn that a crisp mould could no longer be guaranteed, then a new one would be made. Shelley offered his readers some guidance as to how to assmble wood or metal letters on to wooden patterns:

'Soft metal letters are fastened to wooden patterns by means of shellac or small brads. Before an attempt is made to apply the letters to a pattern, their position must be decided upon and lines drawn as a guide for setting the letters. The letters should first be arranged dry for position and spacing, and the position of the first and last letter in each line marked. The letters are then placed face downward on a piece of board and shellacked, as is also the surface to which the letters are to be applied. When the shellac has become quite sticky, the letters should be reapplied and adjusted.'

After the completed master patterns had been used – whether it be single or multiple times – there would have been little need to retain them, so surviving examples are very rare indeed.

One such wooden pattern survives in the collection of the Great Western Trust, (*see previous pages*). It comes, not from the GWR itself, but from the Rhymney Railway in south Wales which became part of the Great Western after the 1921 Railway Act.

It is a remarkable survival and tells us a great deal about how these signs were cast. It was used in the Rhymney Railway's Caerphilly Works – the only locomotive works in Wales – to create the numberplates for their final batch of 'K Class' 0-6-2ST locomotives. They were

SHRINKAGE OF CASTINGS.

The allowance necessary for shrinkage varies for different metals and the conditions under which they are cast. Castings cast under ordinary conditions, where the thickness runs about one inch.

The following allowance can be made:

For Cast Iron,	1-8 inch per foot.
For Brass	3-16 inch per foot.
For Steel,	1-4 inch per foot.
Malleable Iron,	1-8 inch per foot.
Zinc,	5-16 inch per foot.
Tin,	1-12 inch per foot.

Thicker Castings under same conditions will shrink less, and thinner Castings more than this standard.

MAKING CAST-METAL SIGNS

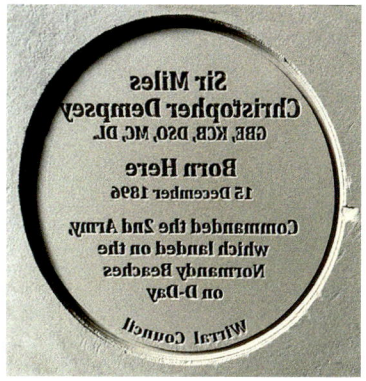
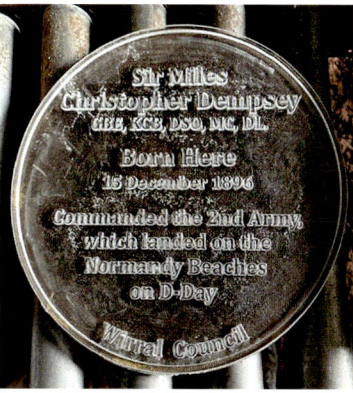

far left: The sand mould for a 'blue plaque' commissioned by Wirral Council, being made at Croft Castings in Whitby. The pattern from which this mould was made was cut using a CNC router. (*Image: Croft Castings Ltd.*)

left: The plaque immediately after being released from the mould, before being cleaned, fettled and painted. (*Image: Croft Castings Ltd.*)

to be numbered 100 to 105 so the central '0' did not need to be moved as each successive sand mould was made.

The basic shape is a piece of 1/4 inch teak, on to which the 1/4 inch thick teak letters and numbers have been screwed or pinned. The holes where the numbers 0 to 9 were pinned in turn can be seen on the baseboard. It is unclear how many times a matrix like this could be re-used. The location of the pinholes show that it was used to cast plates for locomotives with both two- and three-digit numbers. On the back it is identified with inventory No.9362.

Today, simple patterns are more likely to be assembled from metal components rather than wood, with metal letters fixed in place with latex rather than pins or wood glue. This enables easier dismantling of patterns after use. Metal is, of course, much less prone to showing signs of wear, so the individual elements can be re-used many more times than their wooden counterparts. The skills of the pattern-maker, however, are just as important whichever material is being used.

below left and below: Sean Jones, of Jones n Co Cast Metal Designs Ltd in Coventry, assembling the pattern for an address plaque. This requires a good eye and accuracy. The individual letters are fixed in place with latex. After use, the latex peels off easily and every element, once cleaned, can be re-used multiple times.

To illustrate the processes involved, the images on these pages were taken at Jones n Co Cast Metal Designs Ltd in Coventry, a small craft foundry specialising in hand-cast aluminium (and occasionally brass or lead) signs and plaques for private customers worldwide, and for larger clients such as the Duchy of Cornwall. They are all cast from hand-assembled metal patterns.

To make the mould, the completed pattern is laid into what will become the bottom half of the mould – traditionally known as the 'cope' – and covered with fresh moist sand which is evenly tamped down.

In the examples illustrated over the following pages, that sand is

top left: With the patterns laid in the bottom of the frame, Mark Hackett, the moulder, covers them with fresh oil- and clay-rich sand, before the frame is filled with re-used sand.

top right: The sand is tamped down to create a solid, well-packed block.

above: The distinctive colour of Bentomix Petrobond Oil Bonded Metal Casting Sand.

right: Mould-making underway at Carvel Foundry. This small craft foundry produces 200-250 cast plaques a week in a variety of metals for its worldwide clientele.

a mix of sand, clay & (mainly) linseed oil amongst other natural oils, which allows a far finer sand grain to be used. That, in turn, gives a better surface finish. Its commercial name is 'petrobond', or in the case of the sand used at Carvel Foundry, Bentomix - the 'bent' part of the name refers to the sodium bentonite in the clay which acts as the binder, holding the moist sand together in the mould.

The mould is then filled with re-usable black sand which has been suitably moistened, before being tamped down and levelled off.

The skilled mould-maker knows exactly how to turn the mould over safely without damaging it, and remove the pattern, leaving the negative impression of that pattern in the sand, at exactly the depth required for the finished sign. That half of the mould is traditionally known as the 'drag', and it is then turned over so that the pattern can be carefully removed.

In most cases, the back of the sign is usually blank, but in a number of industrial instances it might also carry an inventory number, (*as in the example on page 40*).

top left: The drag is turned over so that the original patterns are now at the top. The surface is dusted with French Chalk.

top right: Preparing to remove the patterns from the drag.

above left: The two moulds, waiting for the cope to be positioned on top of them.

above: Cutting downsprue and riser holes in the cope.

The other half of the mould – which will be positioned on top of the drag – is known as the 'cope', and in order to facilitate easy release of the casting once cooled, both halves are dusted with French chalk or a similar material

Before the two are brought together, holes are made in the cope through which the molten metal is poured. These are known as the feeders and risers. The feeder is obviously where the molten metal is poured in; the risers are where air and gases can escape during the pour, and where the molten metal rises up when sufficient has been introduced. Those feeder holes are also known as the 'sprues' or 'downsprues'.

 Meanwhile, elsewhere in the foundry, aluminium ingots are being melted in an oil-fired crucible ready for pouring. In addition to fresh metal, any signs and plaques which fail quality control are also introduced into the crucible for recycling and re-use – very little goes to waste.

The aluminium most commonly used for small signs and plaques today is known as LM4, a silicon-rich alloy of aluminium and several other metals – 2-4% copper, a maximum of 0.125% magnesium, 4-6% silicon, a maximum of 0.8% iron, 0.2-0.6% manganese, 0.3% nickel, a maximum of 0.5% zinc, and very small amounts each of lead and tin. The copper content gives it a fairly good machinability, and corrosion resistance is quite high.

Aluminium melts at 660°C, lead at 325°C, brass at 900-940°C, and iron at between 1,200-1,550°C, so casting iron depletes the clay and oil content of the sand much more quickly than those other metals.

As the preparation of the moulds is completed, they are laid end to end on the casting floor – a tried-and-tested practice which is probably as old as industrial casting itself – see the Edwardian photograph of the casting floor at the GWR's Swindon Works (*page 101*). This practice minimises the distances which the ladle of molten metal has to be carried and thus makes the job of pouring a lot easier and safer.

While aluminium is relatively lightweight, carrying full ladles of much heavier metals – such as lead or iron – had the potential to be much more hazardous for the foundrymen.

After the metal has cooled down, the drag and cope are separated and the casting released from the sand. Thanks to the French chalk, they separate quite cleanly. The sand can then be broken down, sieved, and re-used several times for other moulds.

Whichever way the master pattern was assembled, it would be made slightly larger than the required size of the finished sign, as every casting

top: The cope, with three holes already bored in it is positioned over the drag, ready for the molten aluminium to be poured.

above: Ingots of the LM4 aluminium alloy used at Carvel Foundry, ready to be melted.

MAKING CAST-METAL SIGNS

above left: The aluminium being melted in the oil-fired crucible in preparation for the pour.

above: The pour – the foundryman carries the filled ladle from one mould to the next, pouring just the right amount of molten aluminium into each, until the overspill appears in the riser holes. The key is doing this as quickly and safely as possible before the metal starts to cool.

left: The acrid smoke of the burning linseed oil and clay as a result of the intense heat of the molten metal.

shrinks slightly as it cools. A skilled foundryman, knowing exactly the cooling characteristics of whichever metal he was using, would have briefed the pattern-maker accordingly, perhaps referring to one of the published tables (*see page 42*). That slight shrinkage also makes it much easier to break the cooled casting out of the sand mould.

The sign itself then has to be 'fettled' – cleaned, polished, powder-coated and painted or, in some cases enamelled, to introduce colour, before joining the countless millions of such signs which have proliferated across the world since those early grave slabs more than 400 years ago.

above. Breaking open the moulds after the castings have had some time to cool down. (*image: John Spear*)

above middle: Separating the still-hot castings from the drags.

above right: The horns where metal has filled up the downsprues and risers, will be cut off using a band saw.

below: The 'fettler', Jo Hackett, uses a range of grinding and buffing tools to smooth out any imperfections in the castings.

The materials may have changed over the years, but the techniques and skills remain the same. In creating signs for the Duchy of Cornwall, Jones n Co Cast Metal Designs Ltd is continuing a practice several hundred years old, but which was given an undoubted publicity boost when, in 1874, Queen Victoria's gardeners ordered the first batch of small cast-metal plant-identification signs, initially for the rose gardens at Sandringham. Two years later the company received its Royal Warrant.

At that time, the company was owned by John Smith, who had taken over a local foundry in Stratford-upon-Avon which had pioneered the making of metal garden labels. With that Royal Warrant, his 'Metallic Label Works', later became known as the Royal Label Factory.

Once its royal patronage became known, the company went on to supply such signs to many gardens and estates, including what is now Forestry England's Westonbirt, The National Arboretum in Gloucestershire, where some of those early labels were rediscovered back in 2007. With the Latin

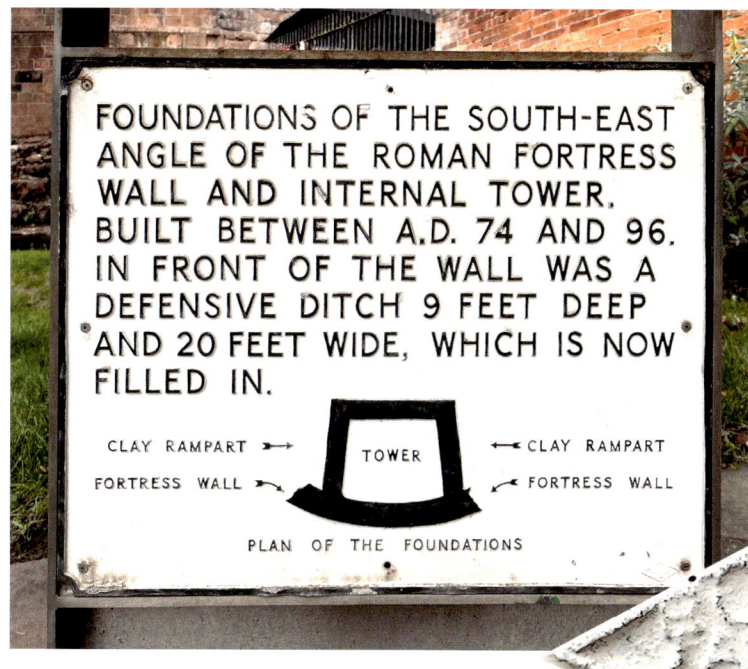

left: A beautifully typeset and finely cast descriptive plaque in cast-iron, marking the remains of the Roman walls in the city of Chester, it was produced for the Office of Works – forerunner of English Heritage – by the Royal Label Factory in the early 1930s. (image: Paul Fox)

below: The logo of the Royal Label Factory, cast into the bottom right corner of the plaque, left. (image: Paul Fox)

plant name on the front, and sometimes also with the maker's name on the back, two moulds would have been required to cast them.

By the 1960s, the company had moved to Chipping Norton and was casting a wide range of road signs and other street furniture, examples of which could be seen all over the Empire and Commonwealth and, in the 1920s, also acquired the contract for the production of cast-iron information boards to be displayed at many of the ancient monuments cared for by what was then known as the Office of Works – later the Ministry of Works, and later still, English Heritage. The company still operates today, and amongst its productions are the National Trust's distinctive marker posts.

below left: Three of the 4-inch by 3-inch cast-iron plant labels rediscovered at The National Arboretum, Westonbirt. From left to right: *Quercus Iberica; Ulnus Young's Weeping; Quercus tinctoria sinuosa quercitron.* The arboretum was created by George Stayner Holford, a landowner and art collector who was the MP for East Gloucestershire until 1872. After stepping down, he indulged his passion for plant collecting, and his aesthetic disposition of those plants and trees around his estate, created a unique landscape. It was he, or his son George, who commissioned the first set of cast-iron plaques from the Royal Label Factory (images: Forestry England's Westonbirt, The National Arboretum)

OUT ON THE OPEN ROAD

The saying 'All roads lead to Rome' is centuries' old, and harks back to the ubiquity of the roads built by Roman engineers – estimated to be around a quarter of a million miles of them – as they expanded their empire across Europe and beyond. But it is one thing knowing that all roads lead to Rome, but quite another knowing how far away Rome is – and that was why the Romans started using marker stones every thousand (mille) double paces. 'Mille' became 'mile' over time, and thus those markers became 'mileposts'. Roman markers were, of course, made of stone, so the first mileposts on Britain's roads were also stone.

Stone marker posts endured for centuries in Britain, being made by the same monumental masons who made tombstones, the lettering being hand-carved into the surface. That was the norm until the closing years

opposite page: A cast-iron 1930s road junction sign displayed in the British Motor Museum at Gaydon, Warwickshire.

below left: This early stone milepost is set into a wall on the A4, London Road, in Calne, Wiltshire.

below: A late 18th century cast-iron plate set into a stone on one of the turnpike roads into Bath, marking the distance from a specific building.

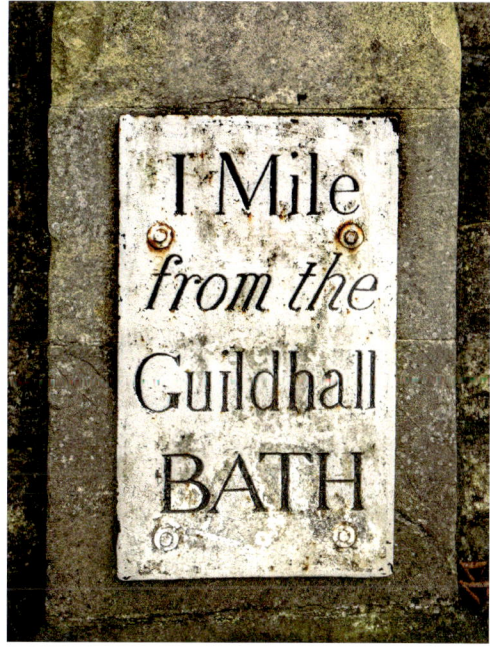

of the 18th century when cast-iron started to replace stone markers as new roads were laid or establish roads improved.

Prior to the first Turnpike Act in 1706, the management and maintenance of roads was the sole responsibility of local parishes and, as a result, travellers could expect to have to endure a wide range of road qualities even on a short journey.

The turnpike system brought with it toll gates and a 'pay per mile' approach to fund-raising in order to improve road quality. Creating each Turnpike Trust, in order to establish the right to charge tolls, required its own Act of Parliament, and by the early years of the 19th century, there were over 1,000 such trusts.

Quite rightly, in return for paying a significant toll, travellers expected a reasonable quality of road surface on which to travel and, as the system evolved, they expected mileposts accurately informing them or their drivers exactly how many more miles had to be covered before they reached their destinations or stopping point.

One of the provisions of some Turnpike Acts was that markers should be placed at mile intervals along each toll road in order to accurately measure the distances travelled. Other Acts simply required that toll-houses and toll gates should be erected every five miles for the collection of those dues.

An interesting difference between 18th century toll roads and those we endure today is that most of the Acts of Parliament which legislated what Trustees of the Turnpike roads could or could not do required that a ticket be issued, valid for 24 hours from midnight – so it was 'pay once and use all day' – a useful dispensation for local commercial carriers and for farmers moving stock around.

Given the intricacy of some of the designs, and the craftmanship of the pattern-makers and evident in many of those markers, it is remarkable – and from an historian's point of view a little irritating – that so few of the foundries identified themselves on their work.

Known makers include Carson and Miller in Warminster, Burt's Foundry in Devizes and the famous Haigh Foundry in Wigan which was established by the Earl of Balcarres, which was also a pioneer in locomotive manufacturing with Robert Dalglish's 'Walking Horse' 0-6-0 locomotive which ran on a local colliery's tramroad in 1812.

Haigh Foundry was, in fact, a complex of three foundries together with a large forge and, long after Dalglish had left the business, the smallest of the three was used in 1837 to make the first cast-iron mileposts for the upgraded turnpike road between Wigan and Preston, the road now known as the A49. Several of those mileposts are still *in situ*. Two different designs were used, but only one of them has the foundry name included in the casting. One was actually stolen a few years ago, but quickly found, the thief dealt with, and the milepost firmly cemented back into its original site.

Another was stolen during the first pandemic lock-down and never seen again. Sadly, reports of historic and iconic mileposts being stolen and sold for scrap are increasing in number.

Several of the mileposts cast by Burt of Devizes remain *in situ*, but despite his name appearing on each of them, little is known about where they were cast. The Burt family were well known in the local area – as 'ironmongers, whitesmiths and bell-hangers' according to an 1811 advertising flyer preserved in the Wiltshire Museum. That flyer marks the business moving from the Lavington area, about five miles south of Devizes, into the town centre

The establishment of the turnpike road between Devizes and West Lavington, shown as 'Lavingt^n' on the left-hand side plate, (*overleaf, bottom left*) was confirmed by a series of Acts of Parliament, the first

opposite page top: A privately-erected, late 18th century milepost, at the junction of the wonderfully-named Charcoal Burner's Road and Salisbury Road through the Savernake Forest, marking distances – in miles, furlongs and yards – to Marlborough Town Hall and Tottenham House, Wiltshire home of the Earls of Ailesbury (later spelled Aylesbury).

opposite page bottom: Very early cast-iron plate from a milepost, originally located about a mile north of Radstock, Somerset, on what is now the A367. It is now displayed in Radstock Museum. It is interesting because of the crudity of its typography, and because the figure '8' is inverted.

below left: Ornate cast-iron milepost erected in 1837 by The Wigan and Preston (South of the Yarrow) Turnpike Trust, on what is now the A49. About six survive between Wigan and Chorley. The foundry name is included in the casting of this post (*image: Duncan Hannavy*).

below: The foundry name did not appear on the less ornate Langtree milepost – which, used to stand near the Boar's Head Inn in Standish, but was stolen during the Covid lockdown in 2020.

in 1751, but these mileposts were probably installed much later – between 1797 and 1840 – that earlier date being when an Act of Parliament enabling a major upgrade to several of the turnpike roads around Devizes was approved, the town being referred to as 'the *Devizes*' throughout the Act. However that later date of 1840 is unlikely as by then the use of 'Sarum' or 'New Sarum' on mileposts had largely been abandoned in favour of 'Salisbury', although, remarkably, the city's name was not *officially* changed from New Sarum to Salisbury until 2009. The 1797 Act charged the Trustees with

'Completing, widening, and keeping in Repair the Road from *West Lavington*, unto and through the Town of the *Devizes*, to the House known by the name of *The Green Man*, in *Seend*, in the County of *Wilts*; and from *Rowde Ford*, through the *Devizes* Market-

place, to join the *Beckhampton* Turnpike Road near *Wansdyke*; and from the East End of the *Devizes* aforesaid, to the Top of Red Hone Hill, in the said County of *Wilts*.'

Further improvements were authorised in 1840, and along those roads, all the surviving mileposts carry the legend 'Burt Devizes'. As the tollhouse which sits at the junction of those three roads, and known locally as 'Shane's Castle', was built between 1830 and 1840, it may not be unreasonable to ascribe a similar date to the mileposts. By that time, George and Henry Burt were located in Devizes Market Place, trading as Ironmongers, Whitesmiths, and Bell-Hangers'

Every local foundryman had his own technique for assembling the master pattern for mileposts, and the Burts' basic technique was to create wooden distance plates which were temporarily fixed to his master pattern before the casting mould was made. Thus, the assembly of the pattern for each milepost, and the changes necessary before the next one was assembled, could be carried out quickly and easily.

As improvements to roads and ease of travel evolved, some of the country's major foundries became involved in casting iron mileposts, – the Stronachlachar post, *below*, was the work of Grangemouth Iron Works which had originally been established in Grangemouth by James McGrouther and Peter Muirhead. The company moved to Falkirk in the early 1900s. Now partly buried in undergrowth, these signs originally stood about three feet tall.

Interestingly, many of the earliest cast-iron marker posts and mileposts used a mixture of upper- and lower-case lettering which, while it was stylistically very attractive, was less legible to passing traffic than markers with the wording all in capital letters. As tolls road brought with them a huge improvement in road surfaces – enabling a considerable increase in speed of travel – legibility became a significant issue.

One of the major figures in the improvement of road surfaces was Thomas Telford, who 'improved' so many of them that he earned the soubriquet 'the Colossus of Roads'. The number of roads and bridges across Britain which can be traced back to his work are in the thousands.

In the late 18th century, he was Shropshire's Surveyor of Public Works, and when he was commissioned to improve the main road from London to Chester, North Wales and across the Menai Strait to Anglesey and the port of Holyhead – the road known today as the A5.

opposite page top: This milestone, from the late 18th century, standing on the B3098 at Styles Hill in Frome, Somerset, combines a cast-iron plate with a stone column. Typical of the period, the lower case 's' had not yet come into common usage, so 'Westbury' reads as 'Weftbury'. By the early years of the 19th century, in most foundries, capitals had replaced the earlier practice of using upper- and lower-case lettering.

opposite bottom left: Cast-iron shell backed by a stone pillar – a milepost on the A360 near Frieth, Wiltshire, by Burt of Devizes.

opposite bottom right: This heavily-eroded Burt post, in the village of St. Edith's Marsh, shows the structure of the cast-iron shell.

below: A late 19th century cast-iron milepost on the road from Aberfoyle to Stronachlachar, at the top end of Loch Katrine a tourist route originally popularised through the early package tours run by Thomas Cook. (*image: John Carruthers*)

He created his own design of mileposts, based on a stone slab not unlike a tombstone, with an inset cast-iron mileage plate bolted to it. All but four of the road's 83 milestones still survive, although a few are slightly removed from their original positions – a remarkable survival rate.

The road was commissioned primarily to appease Irish Members of Parliament who felt cut off from London by the difficulties of the journey they had to undertake. Before the road improvements, it took them several days and involved both coaches and ferries. In 1830 Telford wrote that:

'I never saw a proper milestone that I could copy. I looked for three years all over England trying to find one as a pattern and after all I could not find one that looked like a decent milestone.'

Always a practical man, Telford's design was for a marker stone tall enough to be easily visible to the driver of a passing coach as it sped past. The majority of existing mileposts were less than three feet (one metre) tall, and easily overlooked. The cast-iron distance plate was fixed on to the stone just below the top, setting it between four and five feet above ground level. As road levels have changed over the past two centuries, several are now much lower than they would have been when they were first installed in 1819.

On his North Wales road, the distance to Holyhead was marked in miles on every sign heading towards the port, the other places listed – Capel Curig and Cernioge on the sign – measured in miles and

below: The front face and profile section of Telford's milepost, Plate V in Parnell's book *A Treatise On Roads*. showing how the cast-iron distance plate was affixed to the stone. The bottom two feet would be below ground.

below right: For his mileposts on the A5 road in North Wales, Thomas Telford specified that they should be made from hard Anglesey limestone, almost seven feet tall – the bottom two feet would be below ground –. with large clear lettering on a cast-iron plate, clearly visible from a passing coach. His specification for the signs is detailed and illustrated in *A Treatise On Roads* by Henry Brooke Parnell, published in London by Longman, Rees, Orme, Brown, Green & Longman in 1833.

furlongs – being the nearest inns where the traveller could stop for food and rest and, if necessary with mail coaches, a change of horses.

Heading north-west from Shrewsbury – the town's name In Telford's time was Salop – the first read 'HOLYHEAD 106 – M SALOP 0 M – 6 F'. Much of the road, albeit widened in many places and resurfaced, is still in use today. Perhaps surprisingly, few of the milestones south of Shrewsbury, however, have survived.

Given the proximity of Plas Kynaston to the Holyhead Road project, it is possible that the cast-iron plaques were made by William Hazledine, Telford's 'go to' foundryman. He used the same design on other roads he built in England and across Ireland. Several of these markers still survive.

Hazledine also cast the ironwork for Telford's new bridge which carried the roadway over the Conwy river at Betwys y Coed (*see page 16*). Fittingly, when the Institution of Civil Engineers decided to erect a tribute to Telford at the Welsh end of the road, they replicated his milestone design.

In his published account of his journey through Scotland with Thomas Telford more than a century later, the Poet Laureate, Robert Southey, related a story of some travellers coming south, who were shocked when their horses stumbled and the coach jolted violently as it passed over a succession of potholes. "What's the matter?" one of them asked the driver, who replied "Perthshire—we're in Perthshire, Sir". Perthshire's roads were still notoriously bad at the time, and Telford had recently been appointed by the Road Commissioners to oversee widespread improvements.

The improvements which Telford oversaw did not please everybody, with local blacksmiths complaining that the better road surfaces were ruining their businesses as carriage wheels needed replacing much less frequently. Ah well, you just can't please everyone. Two hundred years later, however, we could still benefit from Telford's 'improvements' today.

above left: Early 19th century cast-iron disc attached to a stone post, one of several of this design on the A673 in Adlington, Lancashire, erected by the Bolton & Nightingale Turnpike Trust. The trust had been established in 1763, but the section between Nightingale crossroads and Bolton was incorporated in 1803. The posts date from that time and the discs were probably cast in Bolton.

above: This curved cast-iron milepost in Milngavie is one of a series erected on what is today known as the A81 road into Glasgow in the early 19th century. The spelling of 'Aberfoil' seen on the milepost – the village is now known as 'Aberfoyle' – was in common usage between 1750 and the end of the 19th century. (*image: John Carruthers*)

A curiosity of many early cast-iron mileposts and plaques is the very specific nature of some of the destinations marked on them – 'Glasgow Royal Exchange', 'Guildhall Bath', 'Frome Market House', are just some of those illustrated on these pages.

But one of the most unusual can be seen set into a wall in the little Wiltshire village of Yatton Keynell where the late 18th century cast-iron plaque set into a wall opposite the village post office marks '97 Miles to Hyde Park Corner' and 'to Sodbury 11', with not a mention of London. One wonders how many of the residents of Yatton Keynell ever went to London, or even knew where Hyde Park Corner was. But for travellers, of course, it was the site of the final toll-gate on their journey to the capital.

It would not be until 1824 that the area between Hyde Park Corner and Constitution Hill was remodelled by Decimus Burton who, between 1826 and 1830, created the open space which would later be dominated by the Wellington Arch.

Several other mileposts on roads leading in to London gave mileages to Marble Arch, however most along the roads to the capital – dating from the early-to-mid 1800s – simply mark distances to London. The reference points for many distance markers would later be General Post Offices.

In addition to mileposts, a completely new marker post –

Some of the many milepost designs to be seen in Wiltshire (*see also pages 52 and 54*).

opposite page: Just past the delightfully-named hamlet of Tiddleywink, this late 18th or very early 19th century cast-iron plaque is built into a wall in the village of Yatton Keynell (known then as Yatton Kenel) near Chippenham. It was installed by the Sodbury Division Turnpike Trust, which had been established in 1751.

left: Octagonal cast-iron plate attached to stone post, on the A361, erected by the Trowbridge Turnpike Trust in 1864.

below left: mid-19th century circular cast-iron plate on rough stone post, erected on Westbury Road, North Bradley (now the A350). Other examples of this design have black lettering on a white ground.

below: Thick cast-iron plate attached to a rough stone pillar near Lacock, Wiltshire, erected in the late 18th century by the Lacock and Blue Vein Turnpike Trust.

top: Three markers side by side on Midford Road, Bath. The Bath Turnpike Trust, first established in 1707, was one of the earliest such trusts in England. Its remit was expanded over the course of the following 200 years and by 1827 the trustees embarked on the erection of cast-iron posts on its major roads. The Bristol Turnpike Trust was established 20 years later in 1727. It adopted the Bath design of mileposts in 1837. Somerset County Council had been established in 1889, and erected boundary markers in 1912, As the Bath Turnpike Trust post illustrated here was a boundary marker rather than a milepost, distances were not included.

above right: Another Bath Turnpike Trust sign, recently restored, this time at Peasdown St. John.

the boundary marker – was introduced in the turnpike era. These marked the limits of a turnpike trust's jurisdiction – on one side of the marker, the upkeep of the road was the statutory responsibility of the trust, on the other it would be the local parish or town council.

It was not unknown for there to be a marked change in road quality as the traveller crossed the line between the two jurisdictions – usually a trust and a parish, as parish councils, just as today, were notoriously short of cash to pay for maintenance.

When the turnpike trusts eventually passed their statutory responsibilities on to county councils or other statutory bodies, new signs were cast, and many still survive.

On a street corner in Bath, for example, three generations of markers still stand side by side – an 18th century milestone, a 19th century turnpike trust marker, and an early 20th century town/county council marker post.

While many early iron mileposts have been swept away over the years as a result of road widening and other improvements, some areas still retain quite a number of them.

In Warminster, Wiltshire, several of them survive, and others of the same design can be found in Frome, Somerset – one, set into a wall on Fromefield, showing 'Bath 13. Frome Market House ½ mile' (*see opposite page*) has been given a date of c.1820 by English Heritage, but was, in fact, erected 20 years later.

These were cast by local iron-founders, Carson and Miller, who operated the Wiltshire Foundry based on the town's East Street. A number of their surviving signs bear the legend 'C & M W 1840', others do not. In total is it believed that at least 26 examples of their Roman pediment design still survive in various states of preservation. When it was being restored by Wessex Archaeology in 2017, the milepost (*overleaf top left & right*), was found to be standing on an earlier stone slab milepost laid flat.

That earlier marker, of course, gave the mileage to 'Sarum' rather than 'Salisbury'.

What is surprising about the proliferation of iron mileposts is the variety of them, with in excess of 100 different patterns seen whilst working on this book – undoubtedly that represents a relatively small fraction of the surviving designs.

Some mileposts in Fife, for example, tell us much more than just mileages, marking a very specific period in Scottish transport history. These beautifully-cast curved cast-iron mileposts marked the 33-mile route from south to north across the county between Pettycur and Newport. They carry the name and date 'Alex. Russell Kirkaldy 1824' and marked a vital stage coach route from Edinburgh to Dundee and Aberdeen.

above left: Boundary marker in Frome, Somerset, marking the boundary between the responsibility of the Frome Turnpike Trust (established 1757) and the parish or town council. The marker probably dates from the 1830s.

above: This milepost stands in Church Street Norton St. Phillips, Somerset, its location reminding us that when it was installed in the early 19th century, even narrow roads through small villages led to London. Like the Burt mileposts (*page 54*) and the Bath Turnpike Trust posts (*opposite*) the design allowed small boards carrying local names and distances to be added to the master wooden pattern as required.

above: The hollow back of a Carson & Miller milepost.

above right: The front of the milepost as restored by Wessex Archaeology.

below: Another C&M milepost erected in 1840 on Elm Hill, Warminster.

below right: This Carson & Miller cast-iron milepost, c.1840, set into a wall on Fromefield in Frome, Somerset, is also Grade II listed. It does not carry the maker's initials or date.

For little more than a decade, Pettycur was the port where ferries to and from ports of the south side of the Firth of Forth arrived and departed. On Fife's northern shore, Newport-on-Tay was where the ferries to and from Dundee arrived and departed.

Pettycur harbour was notorious for silting up and required regular dredging – causing problems as larger vessels were introduced – so, in 1838, the Duke of Buccleugh built a new pier at Burntisland, and the Forth ferries moved their Fife terminus there. A number of new mileposts, with Burntisland replacing Pettycur, were commissioned in 1844 from James Brown & Co., marking the new road across the county.

Elsewhere in Fife, what at a casual first glance might seem multiple examples of the same basic design, turns out on closer examination to be three distinctly different variations cast by the same foundry.

The history of the Fife mileposts benefits from a great deal of research done by local historians over the years, resulting in a database of all the known posts and wayside markers – more than 200 in number in that one county – being published in 2005. Others have been rediscovered since then, and many have been beautifully restored. They are still officially categorised as road signs, so remain the responsibility of Fife Council. A

number of Fife's surviving posts were cast in the early 1850s at the St. Andrews Foundry which was located in Water Street in the town, and had a blast furnace capable of smelting three tons of iron at a time. In 1852 *The St. Andrews Standard* newspaper noted that:

> 'This establishment we are happy to notice is in full and active operation, under the management of its proprietors, our townsmen, Messrs. Alex and John Watson, and the facilities for work in every department of the Iron Foundry, and Blacksmith business, have been greatly increased. The quality of the castings is equal to any imported, and the patterns are of the newest and most improved descriptions. They are constantly casting cooking stoves, Franklins, Patent Windlasses, plough metals, Mill and Ship's castings, etc., which will be furnished at lower prices, than can be imported for. It is as much a duty, as it is our interest, to encourage "home manufactures;" – and we hope that the enterprising Messrs. Watson, will meet with that patronage, which their exertions and workmanship justly entitles them'.

Given the number of their beautifully cast mileposts and direction posts which survive, this aspect of their work was not mentioned by the newspaper – perhaps at that time they had not yet been given the commission.

above left: When first installed, this early milepost stood 3 feet tall, comprising a stone pillar with a cast-iron cap. Over time, some have become partly buried. A date of c.1824 has been suggested, for these markers but they may be a little earlier.

above: One of the Alex Russell mileposts on the Pettycur-to-Newport road. Interestingly, he identified his work on these mileposts as 'Alex Russell 1824 Kirkaldy', mis-spelling the town's name. When the Firth of Forth ferries moved to Burntisland after 1838, new signs replaced 'Pettycur' with 'Bt. Island', followed by the same three destinations – New Inn, Cupar and Newport. Newport continue to be used as the Fife terminal of the Tay ferry service until the Tay Road Bridge opened in 1966.

(*images: Gillian Smith*)

right: The most complex milepost seen in the course of this study, listing mileages to 36 towns and villages. By the 1870s they were re-cycling scrap iron – and reportedly accepting scrap in part payment for new cast objects. Five examples of this pattern of milestone survive. This beautifully cast example stands alongside the B9171, 150 yards from the entrance to Kellie Castle. The typography on some of the other markers produced by this foundry measures distances to eighths of a mile.

opposite top left: This cracked marker post was cast by Robert Douglas of Cupar at his Cupar Mills foundry in the early 1850s Douglas described himself as an 'Engineer' rather than an iron-founder.

opposite top right: For this St. Andrews Foundry variant the hands and distances have been replaced by simple directions – but for Ceres, Cupar, and The Falfields, there is no such guidance. At least six examples of this design survive.

opposite bottom left: On this variant, travellers are offered the pointing hands but no distances. It stands at a junction on the A916 near Pratis House.

opposite bottom right: This milepost – also cast by the St. Andrews Foundry in the early 1850s and mounted on a cast-iron pedestal – has had a chequered history. It disappeared in the 1990s but was returned to its location near Arncroach sometime after 2006. No other examples of this design have been located.

(all images on these pages: Gillian Smith)

The closing years of the 19th and early years of the 20th centuries saw the rise of the motor car – increasing the speed of travel and the distance which could be travelled in a day – bringing with it the introduction of legislation on road usage and protocols.

Central to the regularisation of how people drove their cars was the introduction of cast-iron road signs – initially installed by private motoring and cycling organisations – but by the late 1920s, responsibility had been formally passed to local authorities. That led to a set of standard designs for road signs being introduced, and those designs survived in general use into the 1960s. Many of them can still be found on side roads today.

Taking a driving test in Britain had, remarkably, been voluntary since well before the beginning of the 20th century, but in 1935 it became

compulsory. To draw attention to the new driving era, the first edition of *The Highway Code* had been published four years earlier in 1931, requiring drivers to adhere to the instructions on those newly-installed official road signs.

Quickly into the market for the manufacture of those signs were Pryke & Palmer whose catalogues had, for years, offered an enormous range of cast-iron domestic wares. From the early 1930s their catalogues contained an entire section advertising the full range of road sign – steel pole, hand-painted cast-iron triangle and warning sign, and fitting plate – all for just 5 guineas (£5.5s.0d), or £5.25 in today's money. Allowing for inflation since 1930, that equates to just £331, although one suspects it would cost a great deal more than that today.

All mileposts and milestones were temporarily – and some permanently – removed in 1940 when the risk of invasion was considered imminent. Many were broken up and never replaced, a great loss to history. In some areas, however, they were preserved for the duration of hostilities and re-instated after the war. A number of them, however, were re-erected in the wrong places, and 80 years later some of those location errors have still not been rectified.

With our heavy reliance on satellite navigation today, mileposts and marker posts are no longer the essential travel aids they were as recently as a century ago, and as a result many have been broken, lost or stolen – and surprisingly, thefts continue today. Luckily, however, many of the most important markers, with significant historical relevance, have now been listed and given protected status – not that such protection deters the most determined of thieves. Those which survive are fascinating reminders of times when the world moved at a much gentler pace. Credit must be given to the Milestone Society for their tireless work in identifying, cataloguing and, wherever possible, restoring original markers.

above: A Great Eastern Railway weight limit sign referencing the 1898 and 1903 Motor Car Acts. It was cast in three pieces – the upper 'three' and 'five' are separate inserts. Intriguingly, while most of the lettering is sans serfi, the lower 'Heavy Motor Car, 'Trailer' and 'Five Tons' use sans serif.

above left: The garage number plate on the engine cowling of a 1923 London General bus.

opposite page: A mixture of road and railway signage preserved in the Didcot Railway Centre n Oxfordshire. With reflectors in the red triangle, the level crossing sign is later than that illustrated in Pryke & Palmer's catalogue on p66.

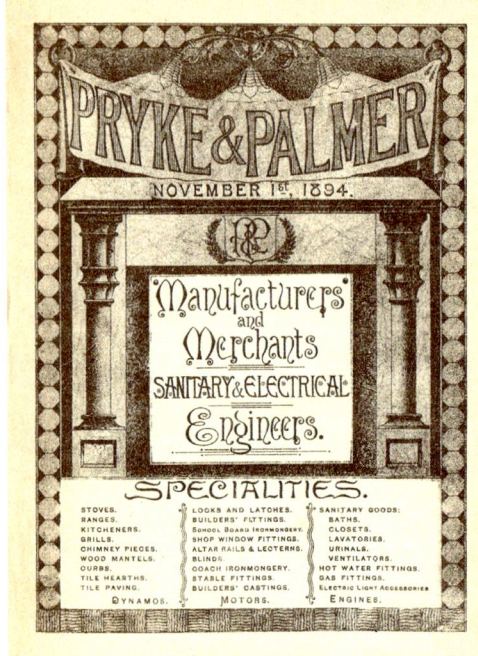
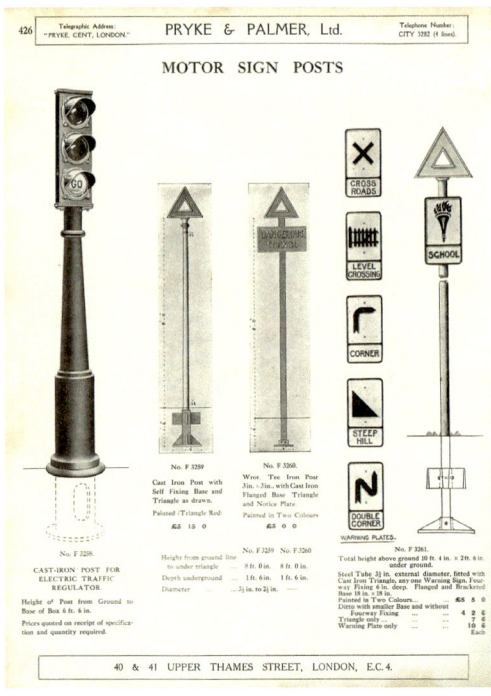

above: Pryke & Palmer's 1894 catalogue was filled, with domestic goods such as cast-iron fireplaces, kitchen ranges and baths.

above right: By 1932. they offered the full range of standard road signs, reflecting the huge surge in demand that had been triggered by the 1930 Road Traffic Act and the introduction of the Highway Code.

right: Still presenting a very traditional look, modern cast metal fingerposts in Corsham town centre, Wiltshire.

In recent years, there has been a revival in the installation of traditional cast-metal signposts, with a number of foundries creating impressive replicas of original designs.

But cast-metal signage was not restricted to roadside architecture – it found its way into the nameplates and model plates affixed to the growing number of motor vehicles using those roads.

Early companies like Albion, Argyll and others all used ornate cast-metal nameplates – individually finished to a very high quality

far left: An early Somerset County Council fingerpost, now at Didcot Railway Centre, Oxfordshire. Posts like this, with their distinctive 'SCC' caps, can still be seen all over the county today.

left: This cast-iron fingerpost in Largo, Fife, has stood without its arms since early in World War 2 when they were cut off, rather than unbolted, to confuse potential invaders. (*image: Gillian Smith*)

below left: Cast metal circular 'Oxfordshire' finial on a fingerpost in the village of Benson.

below: Many Victorian-style cast-iron street signs in Birmingham are, sadly, being replaced with plain modern ones. This example dates from the 1930s when area codes were added.

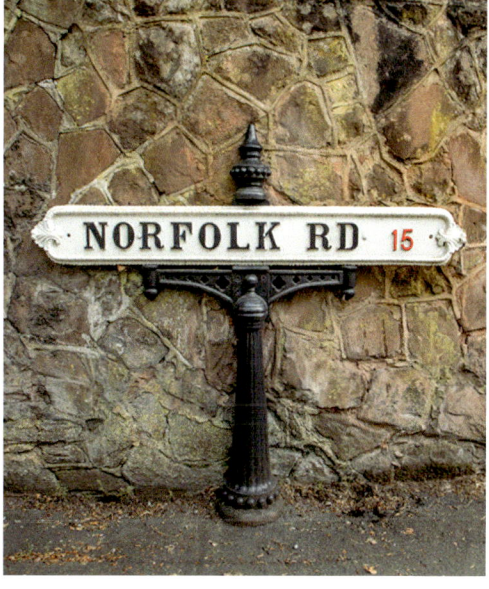

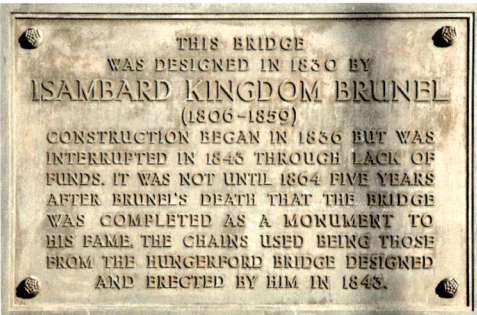

above: The beautifully cast commemorative plaque on Brunel's Clifton Suspension Bridge, Bristol. This plaque is attached to the eastern (Clifton) pylon.

right: On the top of the pylons of Brunel's Clifton Suspension Bridge across the Avon Gorge are two monumental pieces of iron casting. The one on the Leigh Woods (Somerset) side carries the latin legend 'SUSPENSA VIX VIA FIT', which roughly translates as 'A suspended way made with difficulty' – accurately describing the bridge's genesis. The bridge was completed some years after Brunel's deth by John Hawkshaw, President of the Institution of Civil Engineers at the time, and William Barlow. On the Clifton pylon, the casting reads 'COMMENCED 1836 ISAMBARD KINGDOM BRUNEL F.R.S. ENGINEER COMPLETED 1864 JOHN HAWKSHAW F.R.S. WILLIAM HENRY BARLOW. COCHRANE GROVE & CO. CONTRACTORS' The caps were not just decorative – they protected the chain saddles and masonry from erosion due to the elements – something they have successfully done for more than 160 years. Getting those caps up there must have involved some 'difficulty' as well.

– developing, refining and promoting their individual identities, and sometimes even the identities of their component suppliers – the cast sign was ubiquitous. For their luxury 5.6 litre A6 tourer *previous page*, for example, Glasgow-based Albion Motors bought the headlamps from Louis Blériot in Paris – the same man who, at the controls of his Blériot 'Type XI' aircraft on 25 July 1909, became the first person to successfully complete a flight across the English Channel.

In the late 1890s, he had invented the first truly self-contained acetylene headlamps for cars, each with its own internal acetylene generator – giving a much brighter and longer-lasting light than the oil lamps then available – thus capturing much of the early market. Initially it was the profit from his headlamp business which underwrote his experiments in aviation.

Today, sadly, the cost and additional weight of metal manufacture has largely been abandoned, even on premium models, in favour of much cheaper moulded plastic or applied vinyl film.

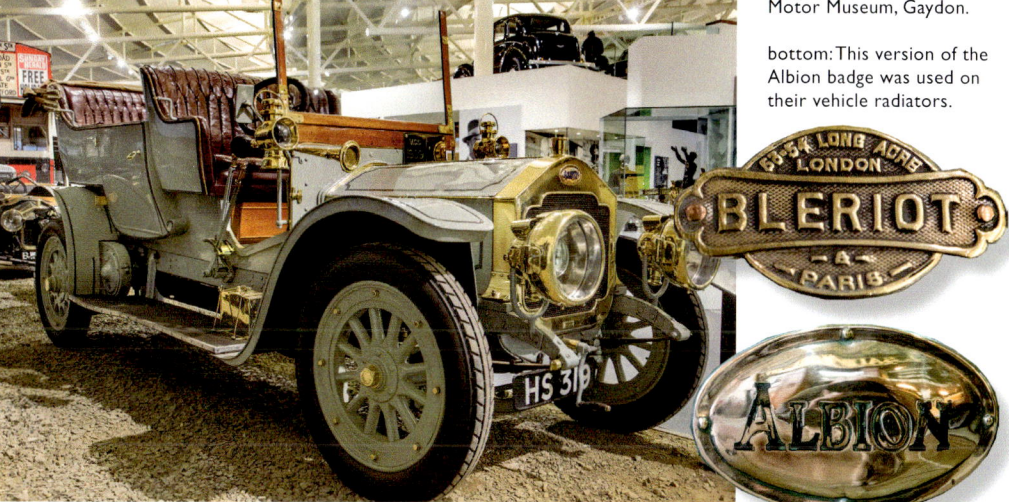

top: Cast-metal badge used on cars by Argyll Motors.

above: The Albion Motors badge from their commercial vehicles.

below: The Blériot badge on the acetylene headlamps fitted to Argyll, Belsize, Panhard and Renault cars, amongst others.

left: A cast-iron road sign, probably late 1920s, seen between Wookey Hole and Easton in Somerset.

below left: A 1909 Albion A6 Tourer in the British Motor Museum, Gaydon.

bottom: This version of the Albion badge was used on their vehicle radiators.

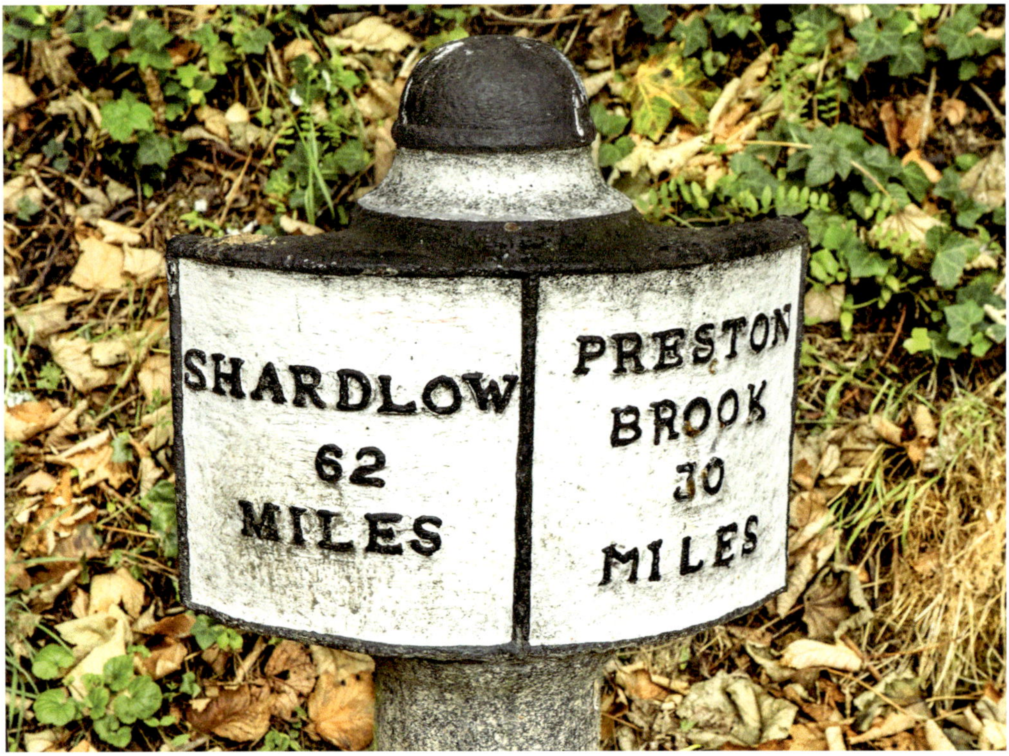
SHARDLOW
62
MILES
PRESTON
BROOK
30
MILES

ELLESMERE
PORT
0 MILES
CHESTER
9 MILES

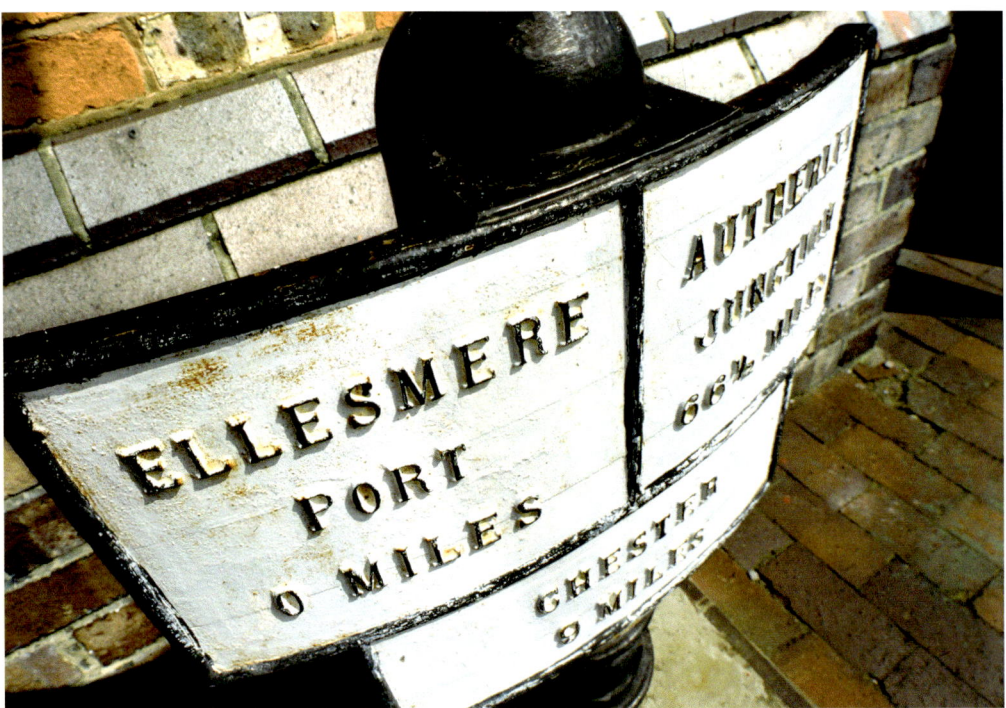

ON THE WATER, AND BY THE WATER'S EDGE

From the closing years of the 18th century, after the initial efforts of James Brindley, Britain's canal systems were evolving into the motorway networks of their day, revolutionising transport, increasing capacity from that of a horse-drawn waggon, and reducing freight costs.

As canals carried more and more freight, it became necessary to measure how far a boat had travelled, and how far it still had to go to reach its destination, or just to reach the next canal interchange. Initially made of carved stone slabs, the milestone, milepost or mile marker became of growing importance to those who lived and worked on the waterways. Later markers had a cast-iron distance plate bolted on to a stone slab, and later still the entire marker post was cast in iron.

opposite top: An 1819 milepost at Harecastle Tunnel, cast by Rangeley & Dixon of Stone, Staffordshire. For its entire length, distances on the mileposts are given to either end of the canal – Shardlow and Preston Brook.

opposite bottom: A milepost of very similar design at Ellesmere Port on Thomas Telford and William Jessop's Ellesmere Canal.

left: The north entrance to Thomas Telford's Harecastle Tunnel on the Trent & Mersey Canal in Staffordshire. The original tunnel by James Brindley, now disused, is to the right, out of the picture.

below: Blue plaques to James Brindley and Thomas Telford at the north entrances to the Harecastle Tunnels. The plaques are cast alluminium.

below: A computer-generated composite image of a replica cast-iron distance plate from the Somersetshire Coal Canal, (now in Radstock Museum) and one of the original stone posts to which it would have been affixed.

bottom: There is now only a short navigable section of the Somersetshire Coal Canal, near the junction with the Kennet and Avon Canal at Dundas Aqueduct.

Amongst early adopters of cast-iron signage were the great engineers John Rennie, Thomas Telford and William Jessop, who located mileposts along several of their canals. Telford was instrumental, in various roles, in the development of a number of the country's canals, and he was a staunch advocate of cast iron, using the material extensively in bridge construction. Just as with his roads, he recognised early on just how important mileposts would be to the canal's busy freight carriers.

Most mileposts are marked with two measures, giving the distances either to the opposite ends of a canal, or to the two nearest major junctions, towns or cities. One exception is the Somersetshire Coal Canal, an important canal, if little known today, which ran from the heart of the Somerset coalfield to its junction with the Kennet and Avon Canal at John Rennie's Dundas Aqueduct in Wiltshire. Rennie was one of the surveyors on the coal canal as well. In its day, this was one of the most successful canals in the country, and by the 1820s was carrying over 100,000 tons of coal per year along its 10.6-mile main line.

The advent of the railway brought about a huge decline in trade, and several sections of the canal were actually repurposed as the route for Great Western Railway branch-lines.

However, it is the canal's mile markers which are of interest here, for they include no names, and only one distance measure each – how many miles still remained to be navigated before reaching the Kennet and Avon junction.

Today only a short section of the coal canal remains navigable where is meets the Kennet and Avon, although several sections have been excavated, revealing, amongst other things, the largest canal basin in England at Paulton. One section has already been returned to water.

Building a canal was an enormous challenge, dependent on accurate surveying, and the subsequent hard graft of the 'navigators' – navvies – who actually dug the channels. But once built, it was every bit as important to maintain these waterways, especially the locks along their routes and the many bridges which passed over them. Thus, early on in the operational life of each canal, a numbering system was introduced to identify each pair of lock gates or bridge so that engineers could quickly reach it and carry out essential maintenance. Lock gates needing repair – either because of damage from boats colliding with them or simple mechanical failure – could immediately bring traffic to a halt, so speed in effecting those repairs was essential.

Taking the Leeds and Liverpool Canal as an example, with its 91 locks and more than 200 bridges, that required a significant number of individually-cast inventory plates.

Mechanical failure of sluice mechanisms or of the gates themselves – often simply due to heavy use for which nobody was to blame – were not uncommon but, of course, there were also signs which listed the responsibilities of boatmen, what they could or could not do, and the penalties if they transgressed.

above: To generations of people on Clydeside, dockside and shipyard cranes are known as 'crans', and this one, fittingly, is known to locals as the 'big cran'. The 150ft high Giant Cantilever Crane – the world's first – was built in 1907 for John Brown's shipyard at Clydebank. It has overseen the building of some of the finest ships ever launched – the *Queen Mary*, the *Queen Elizabeth*, the *QEII*, the Royal Yacht *Britannia* and many others. The winches and drive gear housed at the back of the jib were installed by Stothert & Pitt of Bath, the electric motors by The Lancashire Dynamo & Motor Co. Ltd., of Trafford Park, Manchester, whose maker's plate is illustrated. The silver tower houses a modern lift – out of order on the day of my visit, requiring me to climb the 242-step spiral staircase to the top.

top: A cast-iron numberplate on one of the gates of Lock 42, part of the Caen Hill flight on John Rennie's Kennet & Avon Canal near Devizes, Wiltshire. Several of the locks only have a number viewable as boats head down the flight, but Lock 43 has one on the way up as well. This section of the canal was completed in 1810, but when the iron numberplates were added to the locks is uncertain. Ownership of the canal passed to the Great Western Railway in 1852, and after that date, cast-iron distance markers were introduced. These iron number discs may even date from that period as well. Why there is a full stop after the numbers on every lock gate is unknown.

right: On James Brindley's South Oxford Canal, each of the many bridges has a cast numberplate. Several bridges have been replaced by the Canal & River Trust with replicas of Brindley's 1770s. design. Bridge 219, near Shipton-on Cherwell, dates from 2022. His cost-saving design was for counter-balanced wooden bascule bridges at little-used crossing points. When the first cast-metal plaques were added is unknown. The default position for these little-used bridges was 'open'.

The canal system was hugely dependent on a constant supply of water to keep locks full, and thus to keep boats on the waterway moving. On many canals, it was equally dependent on powerful pumping engines to deliver that water to the higher levels – thus enabling cargo boats to sail over hills. Those engines were, of course, all given inventory numbers by the canal companies – usually cast-iron or cast-brass, and the engine builders usually ensured that their makers' plates were in prominent view, should any fellow canal owners in search of pumping engines be given access to the engine house and be impressed by what they saw.

What had become commonplace on mill engines, was mirrored on ships, with makers' plates additionally carrying yard numbers and build dates. The practice of mounting makers' plates continues today.

Of course, today with heritage groups driving the restoration of the remains of our industrial history, it is sometimes difficult to confirm that the signage on preserved machinery is appropriate. One instance where, for a time, it was not, is Brunel's SS *Great Britain*, once the largest steamship in the world, built in Bristol in 1843 and rescued from Sparrow Cove in the Falkland Islands in 1970.

By 1983, the ship, sitting in Bristol's Great Western Dry Dock where it had been built – having been given a cosmetic external restoration while work continued within – carried cast lettering on her stern which identified her as *The Great Britain*, a name she had never carried during her working life.

above left: The St. Helens Canal was opened in 1757 as the Sankey Canal, and in 1845 ownership passed to the St Helens & Runcorn Gap Railway, later part of the London & North Western Railway. The bridges were either bascule 'drawbridge' type or swing bridges to enable tall-masted sailing craft to use the canal unimpeded. The right to levy fines dates from an Act of Parliament passed in 1822.

above: The weight of 'the ordinary traffic of the district', must have been clear to the Victorians, as this wording was used by many canal and railway companies without further explanation.

below left: A replica cast-metal Leeds & Liverpool Canal plaque.

below: A cast-iron plate on a marker post on the Leeds & Liverpool Canal at Top Lock near Wigan.

right: As recently as 1999, when wooden lock gates on the Leeds and Liverpool Canal were being replaced by steel gates, the tradition of cast-metal plaques was being maintained with the introduction of date plates. These are the gates at Deane Locks near Wigan., Lancashire

below right: The cast metal inventory plate on bridge 69 on the Leeds and Liverpool Canal, also near Wigan, seen through the arch, while the bridge's completion date is commemorated in stone either side of the keystone.

below: Armstrong's maker's plate on one of the steam engines which powered the hydraulic systems in the docks at Ellesmere Port, where the Ellesmere (Shropshire Union) Canal meets the River Mersey.

bottom right: The restored pair of duplex cross-coupled Armstrong engines at Ellesmere Port, installed in 1873, could pump 56 gallons a minute, creating the 750psi needed to operate the docks' hydraulics.

top: The cast-iron Boulton & Watt beams possibly bought second-hand for John Rennie's water-powered Claverton Pumping Station near Bath which raised water from the River Avon to the Kennet & Avon Canal. On the wall behind the beams are five of the original lock gate numberplates, preserved when the wooden gates were replaced with steel.

below: The cast-metal numberplate on one of the Claverton beams. The GWR had taken over the canal in 1852, so this might be their inventory number.

At the time of her launch in 1843 – and in illustrations depicting that launch – she was referred to as *The Steamship Great Britain*, but her launch name was *Great Britain*. She is now known as 'Brunel's SS *Great Britain*, but as the prefix 'SS' – meaning 'steam ship' – did not enter common usage until a few years later, she was simply known as *Great Britain* – the name she once again carries on her stern.

The ubiquity of cast metal signs over the past two centuries meant they did not just appear on ships – they were also to be found on the many aids to shipping which were introduced across the centuries.

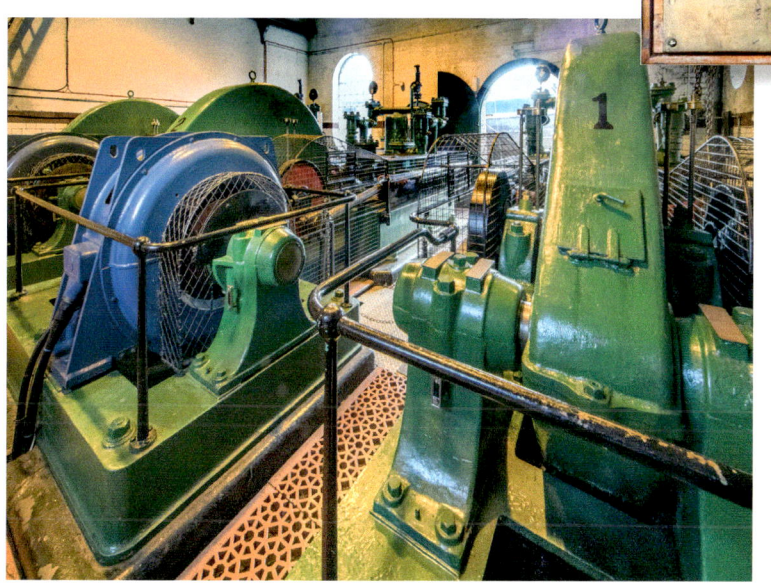

left: The Underfall Yard Engine House in Bristol's Floating Harbour has 1907-built electric pumping engines by Fullerton, Hodgart & Barclay of Paisley which created the hydraulic pressure for the Armstrong, Whitworth system which powered the swivel bridge, the lock gates and some of the dockside cranes as well. These replaced the original steam engines which had been installed in 1887.

above: Fullerton, Hodgart & Barclay's cast-metal maker's plate on the Underfall engines.

above: William Fairbairn's patented design for a rotating quayside steam crane revolutionised the loading and unloading of vessels by enabling cargo to be transferred directly from a ship's hold to waiting railway waggons. This example, built by Stothert & Pitt of Bath in 1878, is on Bristol's Floating Harbour and is still occasionally steamed. The manual points lever in the foreground is by Tyer & Co. Ltd. of London and Carlisle. The company built a wide range of railway signalling equipment, some of it under licence from the Great Western Railway, other licensed from Swiss manufacturers.

above right: The Stothert & Pitt maker's plate on the jib of the crane.

Seven hundred and fifty miles north of Bristol, the giant red foghorn at Sumburgh Head lighthouse on Shetland's Mainland was installed in 1905-06, and although it is no longer used for the benefit of shipping, it is the only fully-functioning foghorn left in the British Isles. Modern navigation aids such as radar, and closed bridges on ships, meant that they had become much less important than in the past.

As a child in the 1950s, I remember the booming sound when fog regularly engulfed the Scottish east coast villages where we spent summer holidays.

Originally, the engine house was equipped with Crossley paraffin engines, and they created compressed air at the 25psi necessary to operate the foghorn. Those engines operated for almost 45 years until replaced in 1950-51 by the Glasgow-built K2 Series Kelvin Diesels, built at their Dobbie's Loan, factory, which can still be seen in the engine house today. They in turn drove compressors built by Alley & McClellan at their Sentinel Works in Polmadie, also in Glasgow.

The foghorn and its engine room were restored to their operational state in 2015, and now form a fascinating part of the visitor experience.

On ships themselves there could be dozens of cast metal 'maker's plate', for the engine-makers, the winch-maker, the company which

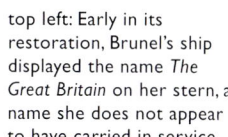

top left: Early in its restoration, Brunel's ship displayed the name *The Great Britain* on her stern, a name she does not appear to have carried in service.

top right: Taken 30 years later, this image shows the stern with the correct name displayed.

above: The replica maker's plate on Isambard Kingdom Brunel's steamship, SS *Great Britain*. The Great Western Steamship Company's first successful trans-Atlantic vessel, the *Great Western*, had been launched in 1838.

above left: The world's largest iron ship, when launched, the restored SS *Great Britain* in Bristol's Great Western Dry Dock where she was built.

left: Modern cast signpost, at Brunel's SS *Great Britain,* shows the mileages to the ports to which she sailed, and to the Falklands where she lay beached in Sparrow Cove for decades.

top left: The 1820-built 56ft high tower of Sumburgh Lighthouse, Shetland, was built by Robert Stevenson.

above: Pointing south out to sea, Sumburgh's foghorn was installed by James Dove in 1906.

top right: Dove's brass plate is all that survives from the 1906 installation.

above right: Unusually the maker's plates on Sumburgh's Kelvin K2 diesel engines are not in a prominent position.

made the steering gear, the deck cranes and so on. For example, the SS *Shieldhall*, part of the bridge steering mechanism for which, *illustrated above*, had a total of 22 steam engines controlling its various functions, a number of which provided power for the steering system itself. Each of those would have had its own maker's plate.

Big ships had big heavy rudders, and whereas steering HMS *Warrior* – which reportedly was very difficult to steer because of her weight – required 16 crewmen to turn the giant steering wheels which controlled the rudder, *Shieldhall*'s power steering could be controlled by one man.

On every ship there would, additionally, be label plates on levers and other control systems to aid the crew. In engine rooms – which were potentially dirty and oily – only metal plates would survive the continuous cleaning and polishing which was the norm in steamships.

John McGregor & Co's Dunedin foundry on New Zealand's South Island built everything from the cast-iron stove preserved in Arrowtown school, *inset*, to the 330grt twin-screw steamer TSS *Earnslaw*, *left*, seen here on Lake Wakatipu.

below left: PS *Wingfield Castle* and her maker's plate, *inset*. She served for 40 years between 1934 and 1974 as one of the Humber ferries, util withdrawn when the Humber Bridge was opened. She is now preserved in Hartlepool.

Thus, their importance in aiding safety cannot be over-stated. There was minimal opportunity for confusion with such durable signs and labels.

In the case of heritage vessels, additional commemorative plaques have been added over the years to mark significant anniversaries. Collectively they constitute a unique visual commentary in cast metal on the life of each vessel, and the involvement of the many companies involved in the building, modification, and maintenance of a ship in its working life.

below: Cast metal plaque added to TSS *Earnslaw* in 1990 to mark New Zealand's 150th anniversary.

bottom: Winches and capstans for the TSS *Earnslaw* were manufactured and supplied by Emerson Walker & Thompson Bros Ltd of Gateshead and London.

Those standard and finish of the castings for plates and signs, whatever their purpose, epitomise the pride in quality manufacturing which helped Britain become such an industrial powerhouse. We are so used to signage today that hose plates now probably have less impact than they did in their heyday, but their importance our industrial narrative is immense.

left: Donkin & Co. Ltd. began manufacturing ship's steering gear in Walkergate, Newcastle, in 1879. By the mid 20th century their equipment had been installed in more than 12,000 ships.. This cast brass direction indicator on the 1,792grt SS *Shieldhall*, built in 1955 in Renfrew, Glasgow, by Lobnitz & Co.

clockwise from below: The 1904 engines on PS *Kingswear Castle*: the engine-maker's plate: PS *Kingswear Castle*, built in Dartmouth by Philip & Sons in 1924, now back sailing on the River Dart.

opposite page top left: The bell on HMY *Britannia* was cast in 1953 by Mears & Stainbank of Whitechapel.

top right: The 6-inch gun on HMS *M33 (Minerva)*, the only surviving vessel from the Gallipoli Campaign in 1916, is an Armstrong Whitworth Mk.XVII originally from the Chilean battleship *Almirante Latorre* built by Armstrong at Elswick on the Tyne.

middle left: HMS *Alliance* is now preserved at the Museum of the Royal Navy in Gosport, Hampshire.

middle right: The replica brass facing rim on the restored HMS *Warrior*'s quarter-deck steering rig recalls a signal sent to the ship by Princess Alexandra of Denmark in 1863 after the vessel escorted the royal yacht *Victoria and Albert* on which she was travelling to Britain to marry the Prince of Wales, the future King Edward VII. This casting dates from the ship's 1980s restoration.

bottom left & right: Cast metal signage abounds in the engine room of HMS *Alliance*.

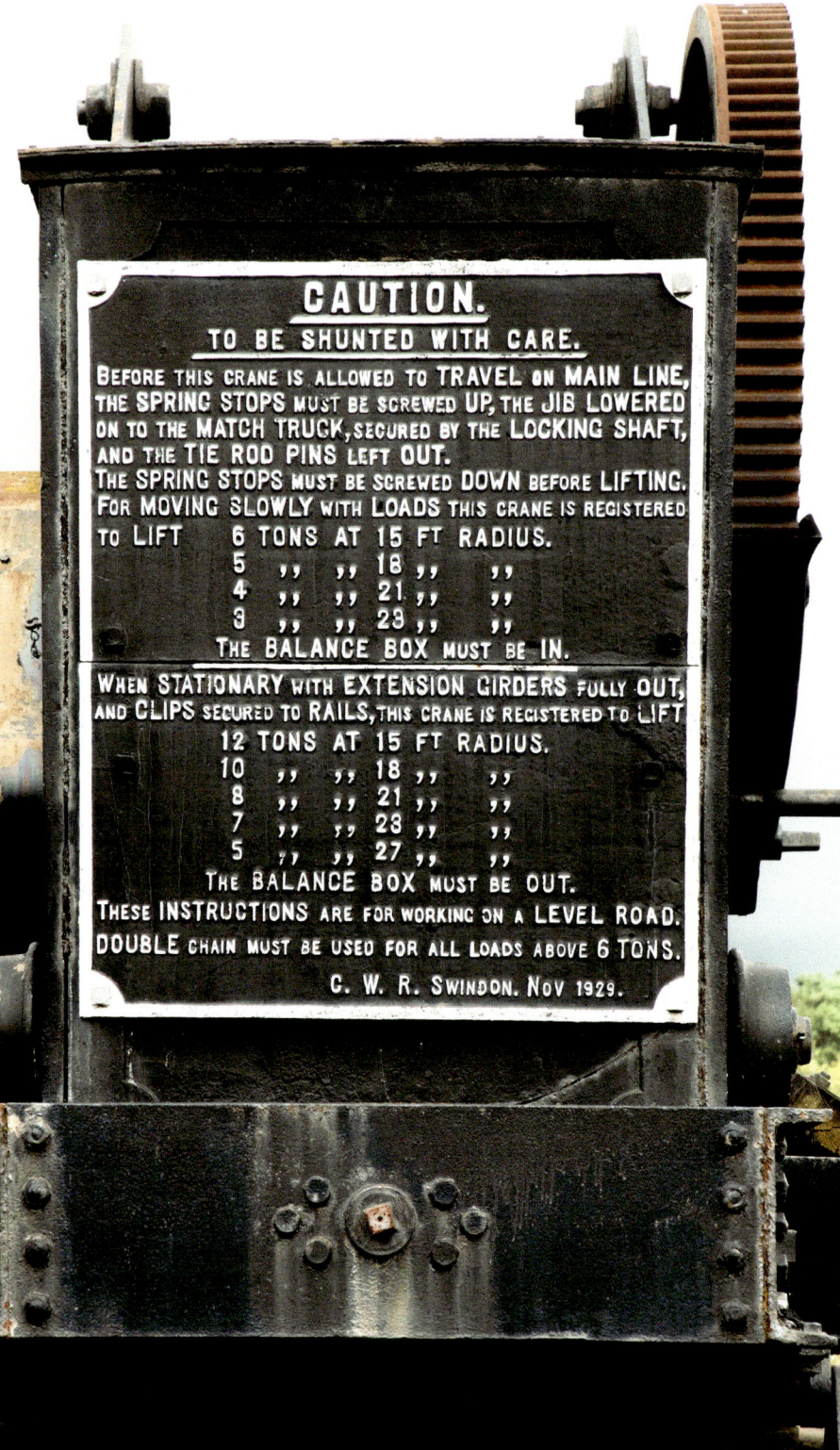

CAUTION.
TO BE SHUNTED WITH CARE.

Before this crane is allowed to TRAVEL on MAIN LINE, the SPRING STOPS must be screwed UP, the JIB LOWERED on to the MATCH TRUCK, secured by the LOCKING SHAFT, and the TIE ROD PINS left OUT.
The SPRING STOPS must be screwed DOWN before LIFTING.
For MOVING SLOWLY with LOADS this crane is registered to LIFT   6 TONS AT 15 FT RADIUS.
    5 ,,   ,, 18 ,,   ,,
    4 ,,   ,, 21 ,,   ,,
    3 ,,   ,, 23 ,,   ,,
The BALANCE BOX must be IN.

When STATIONARY with EXTENSION GIRDERS fully OUT, and CLIPS secured to RAILS, this crane is registered to LIFT
    12 TONS AT 15 FT RADIUS.
    10 ,,   ,, 18 ,,   ,,
     8 ,,   ,, 21 ,,   ,,
     7 ,,   ,, 23 ,,   ,,
     5 ,,   ,, 27 ,,   ,,
The BALANCE BOX must be OUT.
These INSTRUCTIONS are for working on a LEVEL ROAD.
DOUBLE CHAIN must be used for all LOADS above 6 TONS.

G. W. R. SWINDON. Nov 1929.

RAILWAY SIGNAGE – NAMES, NUMBERS AND INSTRUCTIONS

The railways were early adopters of cast metal for just about every sign they needed – from the very large instruction set on the GWR's 12-ton travelling crane, opposite, to the very small plaques on the levers in signal boxes, below. Their use of cast metal nameplates and numberplates is almost, but not quite, as old as the railways themselves, and certainly pre-dates the use of metal signage on stations and by the trackside, where wood prevailed on many lines well into the 20th century. The durability of metal over wood, and its resistence to British weather, made it the obvious choice for those railway companies either with their own locomotive works and foundries, or those with local access to such facilities.

In the 1831 book Coloured Views of the Liverpool and Manchester Railway – from Drawings made on the spot by Mr. T. T. Bury, published by R. Ackermann, some locomotives are shown with their names painted on to the wooden boiler cladding, others with no identification at all. Two plates added in the 1833 edition show locomotives 'Liverpool' and 'Fury' with cast metal nameplates.

opposite page & above: The cast-iron 'instruction set' fixed in 1929 to the rear of the 1894 Swindon-built Great Western Railway 12-ton travelling Hand Crane, now at Didcot Railway Centre.

below and inset: The cast brass label plaques on the 26-lever signal frame in the restored Carr House signal box at Rowley station in the Beamish Museum.

The Liverpool & Manchester Railway's 2-2-0 'Planet Class' locomotive *Fury*, designed by Robert Stephenson and built by Fenton, Murray & Jackson in Leeds in 1831, was one of of that company's earliest locomotives to be fitted with cast-metal nameplates. This illustration comes from the n1833 edition of Ackermann's book *Coloured Views of the Liverpool and Manchester Railway – from Drawings made on the spot by Mr.T.T. Bury,*

Robert Stephenson's 0-4-0 locomotive *Locomotion* – the No. 1 engine, on the Stockton and Darlington Railway and the first in the world to haul a passenger train – was built in 1825 and was unofficially named *Active*. It was heavily modified in 1846 and fitted with the wheels seen in this Edwardian postcard to improve its traction. It was taken out of service in 1856 and preserved. It was subsequently given the new cast metal nameplate seen here incorporating the date '1825' below its name, and displayed at Darlington Station from 1892 to 1975.

The nameplate on Stephenson's 1825-built locomotive, *Locomotion* as preserved today. It is widely believed to have been the first locomotive to have carried a cast-metal nameplate, and this simple design is believed to replicate the original. It is now part of the National Collection at Shildon, while a working replica can be seen at Beamish Open Air Museum in Northumberland.

In the early years of railway development, nameplates were usually the only identifiers – very few of the early locomotives were given fleet or class numbers. An exception was the Stockton & Darlington Railway whose first engine, *Locomotion No.1*, carried both name and number. Given that precedent, it is perhaps surprising that the protocol was not immediately adopted by other companies as they began operations – without numbers, the potential for confusion could have become an issue. For example, by 1829 when Stephenson's *Rocket* first ran on the Liverpool and Manchester Railway, there was another locomtive – *Rocket No.7*, built by Stephenson in 1827, already running on the Stockton & Darlington.

But once fleets expanded, cast metal plates proliferated to include nameplates, numberplates, shed plates and removable cast header boards, identifying particular services rather than specific.

below left: The painted cast-metal nameplate on the 0-4-2 *Lion*. Built for the Liverpool & Manchester Railway by Todd, Kitson & Laird of Leeds in 1838, it was one of six constructed under Robert Stephenson's patents. In 1953 it briefly became famous again as *Thunderbolt* when temporarily fitted with a new nameplate, as the star of the Ealing comedy 'The Titfield Thunderbolt'. Now preserved in the Museum of Liverpool, it is seen here during 'the Rocket 150' celebrations at Rainhill in 1980.

bottom left: The cast-brass nameplate on the replica of Stephenson's 1829-built *Rocket* which was built to run on the Liverpool & Manchester Railway. *Rocket* famously took part in the 'Rainhill Trials' in 1829 and in some illustrations, when new, the locomotive carried no nameplate.

below: The replica of Timothy Hackworth's *Sans Pareil* – seen here getting up steam at Rainhill in 1980 – has a cast brass nameplate mounted on a woodplinth.

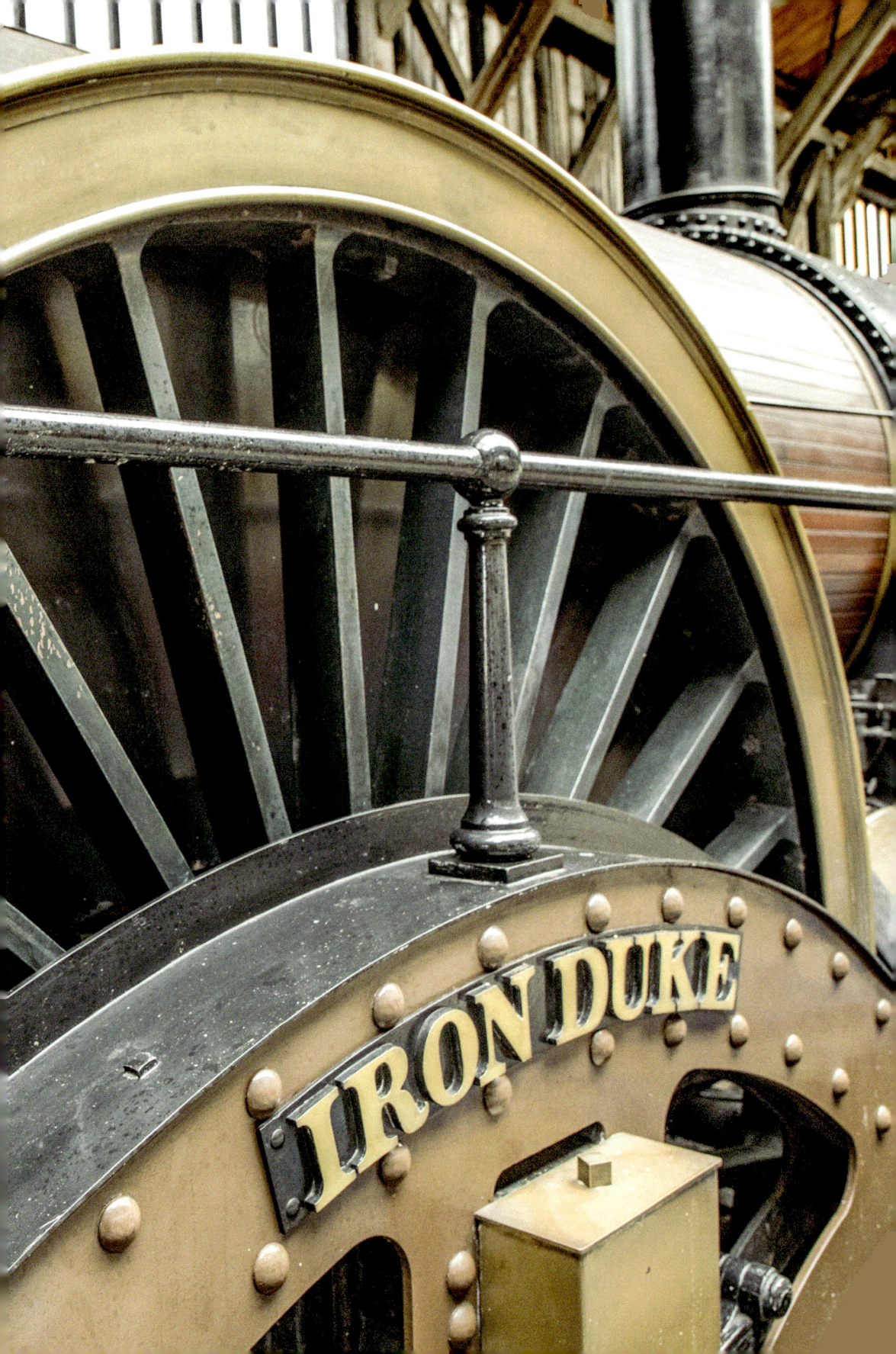

left: The replica of the Great Western's *North Star* at 'Steam' in Swindon has its name spelled out in individually cast letters. The 'Star Class' 2-2-2 broad gauge locomotives, designed by Robert Stephenson, were built to haul passenger trains and were introduced into service over a three-year period starting in November 1838. They were withdrawn between April 1864 and September 1871. *North Star* was the GWR's first locomotive.

below left: Designed by Daniel Gooch and built by Jones, Turner & Evans of Newton-le-Willows in Lancashire in 1840, *Fire Fly* had its name cast on two metal plates. This working replica was built in 2005 by the Fire Fly Trust at Didcot

Cast-iron nameplates were probably initially adopted on locomotives and rolling stock as an early form of corporate branding – long before such terminology became part of common usage – and to give the machines a less threatening aura. Some companies consistently used the same typeface for decades on their locomotives' nameplates.

above: Cast-metal GWR crest, on preserved Class 57 diesel *Pendennis Castle*.

opposite page: The original *Iron Duke* was the first locomotive to be out-shopped from the GWR's Swindon Works in 1846. Designed by Daniel Gooch, the rigid 4-2-2 configuration was an unusual feature of the design. In 1985, a replica *Iron Duke* was built to mark the 150th anniversary of the GWR. It uses parts from two ex-LNER J94 'austerity' tank engines.

above right: Now carrying four cast-metal name and number plates, and a cast Furness Railway Trust headboard, Furness Railway 0-4-0 No.20 was built at Sharp, Stewart & Company's Atlas Works in Manchester in 1863 and is said to be the oldest operational steam locomotive in Britain. While 'No.20' on the buffer bar is in individually hand-cut brass letters and numbers screwed in place, the numberplates on the sides of the boiler and the maker's plates on the cab sides, are in cast brass.

below: Furness Railway 0-6-0 No.3, known as *Coppernob* – built in Liverpool in 1848 by Bury, Curtis & Kennedy – is preserved in the National Railway Museum, York.

As each railway company's holdings expanded, an effective inventory system to keep control of it all became essential. Identifying locomootives by their name alone was all very well when there were just a few of them, but as stock lists expanded exponentially, a numbering system was inevitable.

In the case of the Great Western Railway, it seems locomotive numbering started around the time the conversion from broad-gauge to standard-gauge was being planned. Initially, that was a simple numeric sequence, starting at '1', but by the time the first 1,000 had been numbered, the limitations of such a system were becoming apparent.

And as numbers expanded yet further, the 'class' system evolved making identification of a specific locomotive, or spares for that locomotive, more straightforward. And how better to identify those locomotives than with cast-iron numberplates.

As tenders and rolling stock were interchangeable, they too were given inventory numbers, and cast-iron plates as well.

Every time the numbering system was expanded, the men in the pattern shop and foundry were tasked with making replacement numberplates.

A number of the smaller companies – such as the Rhymney Railway for example (*see pages 40-41*) – stayed with simple numerical sequencing, the locomotive numbers only needing to be changed when they were absorbed into larger groupings. By the end of the 19th century, the number of cast-metal plates being carried around the country on locomotive and rolling stock was in the millions, and as track speed increased, the legibility of those numberplates, rather than their aesthetics, became an issue.

It was already widely recognised that 'sans serif' typefaces were more instantly readable than 'serif' – such typefaces originally being referred to as 'Grotesque' or 'Gothic' but becoming more widely appreciated for their legibitiy with the introduction of sans serfi printing type by William Caslon in 1745.

The use of sans-serif capital letters on numberplates for both locomotives and rolling stock was widespread by the 1870s and '80s – *see above and below* – and a useful side-effect of that change was that the hand-cut masters of the sans-serif letters used by the pattern-makers proved to be much more durable than the more elaborate serif faces.

The London Underground system was an early 20th century adopter of sans-serif typeface for its corporate identity, commissioning its own typeface from designer Edward Johnston in the years before the First World War. One of Johnston's team was a young monumental mason by the name of Eric Gill, whose eponymous typeface would first appear in

above left: The sans-serif typeface on the nameplate on the LNER A3 Pacific, No.60103 *Flying Scotsman*, in her current Brunswick Green livery.

above: Photographed in 1967 in Manchester's then-derelict Liverpool Road Station, this abandoned L&YR fines book listed countless 'offences' committed by employees. I wonder what happened to it?

below: With an oversize cast-metal nameplate, the 2-cylinder 2-2-2 *Dwarf* was built at George England's Hatcham Iron Works for the London & Blackwall Railway in 1849, and cost £1000. *Dwarf*, through several owners, ended her working life hauling an inspection coach on the London & North Western Railway.

bottom left and right: Taff Valley Railway cast-iron numberplate and maker's plate, probably from a wooden-sided freight wagon made at the railway's Cathays Works in Cardiff in June 1893. These plaques measure 12 inches (30.5cm) and 8 inches (20.3cm) across respectively

right: Didcot Railway centre is home to several locomotives which have made near-miraculous returns from the dead – none perhaps more so than 'King Class' No.6023 *King Edward II*, one of the best-looking and most powerful class of locomotives the GWR ever built. It was not rescued until 1985 – after spending 23 years in the Barry scrapyard – and reconstructed over a period of nearly another 25 years. No.6023, was built at Swindon Works in 1930, withdrawn in 1962.

middle: The nameplate above the splasher on the 1931-built GWR '4900 Class' locomotive No.5900 *Hinderton Hall,*now at Didcot, uses the typical GWR typeface,

below right: No.7821 *Ditcheat Manor.* Although known as a GWR '7800 Class' locomotive, 7821 was actually built by British Railways at Swindon in 1950 and is now back where she was built The red background was introduced early this century, replacing the conventional black ground.

below: A combined name and numberplate from the 1900-built 'Bulldog Class' locomotive *Tregeagle* using both serif and sans-serif typefaces. displayed at Didcot Railway Centre.

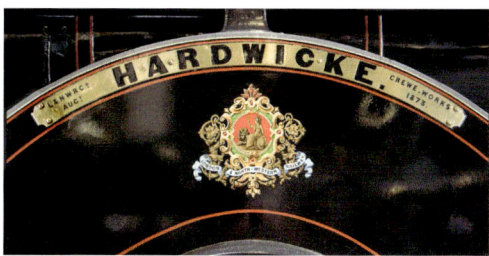

the 1920s and achieve widespread acclaim for its simplicity of design and excellent legibility. The similarity with Johnston's original is obvious.

'Gill Sans', as it became known, would be adopted by several railway companies as the standard for much of their more utilitarian signage, the more elaborate serif faces continuing to be used by many for locomotive nameplates.

The most widely used of those faces was 'Clarendon' – one of a group of fonts widely referred to as 'Egyptian' – designed in 1845 by William Thorowgood & Company of Fann Street Foundry in Aldersgate Street, London. The font became so heavily associated with the GWR that a variation of it became known as 'Swindon Normal'.

Even then, there were exceptions, as some combined name and number plates – such as the 1900-built 3359 Tregeagle – used a combination of both 'serif' and sans-serif lettering and numerals.

While the GWR remained loyal to serif faces after grouping, the other 'big three' – the Southern, the London Midland & Scottish, and the

top left : The nameplate on the London & North Western Railway's 1873 locomotive *Hardwicke*, built at Crewe Works in August 1873.

above: With the typography of its nameplate in keeping with the traditional GWR house style, 4-6-0 'Saint Class' locomotive No.2999 *Lady of Legend,* was built between 2009 and 2019 at the Didcot Railway Centre, to a design by George Jackson Churchward – the original numbering of 'Saint Class' locomotives stopped at 2998. *Lady of Legend* was built using the frames and boiler of No.4900 'Hall Class' No. 4942 *Maindy Hall.*

left: A fine example of casting – the nameplate on Southern Railways 'Schools Class' locomotive No.925 *Cheltenham*, built at the railway's Eastleigh Works in April 1934. Photographed on the Mid-Hants Railway

left: Sans serif lettering on the nameplate of LMS 'Princess Royal Class' locomotive No.6201, *Princess Elizabeth.*

The cast-metal 'sans serif' nameplate on the LNER's Gresley-designed *Mallard* standing alongside the LMS Stanier-designed streamlined *Duchess of Hamilton* in the National Railway Museum, York.

0-6-0ST No47, *Moorbarrow* at Cranmore Station on the East Somerset Railway. The locomotive carries several cast plates – name plates either side of the boiler, Robert Stephenson & Hawthorns Ltd. maker's plates on the bunker, and a 1955 Railway Executive registration plate on the cab side – number 167s. Built in 1955 for the National Coal Board, after a spell on the East Somerset, it is now on the Gwili Railway in Wales. It was given the name *Moorbarrow* some time after 1973 when it was preserved.

London & North Eastern railways – all adopted 'sans-serif', the first being the LNER which standardised specifically on 'Gill Sans' across the board in 1926.

While the Great Western consistently used curved nameplates above the splashers, the other three big companies varied the positions of their locomotive names, some above the splashers, others at various positions along the sides of the boiler casings, or on the smoke deflectors.

left: Completed in 1887, *Lindsay* is the only surviving locomotive, built by the Wigan Coal & Iron Company at their Kirkless workshops. It was built for work at the Earl of Balcarres and Crawford's Standish Collieries. Lindsay is the family name of the Earls of Crawford. The plaque on her cab side was added on her 100th birthday in 1987 when this photograph was taken. The 138-year-old locomotive is currently undergoing a major restoration prior to being returned to steam.

opposite page: British Railways Class 2MT No.46512 arriving at Boat of Garten on the Strathspey Railway. It carries the BR shed code 60B for Aviemore and Boat of Garten.

This page, clockwise from top left:

Southern Railway 'U Class' No.31806 at Norden Station on the Swanage Railway. It carries the plate, 71B. for Swanage Shed.

British Railways Standard Class 4, No.80104 at Swanage station – it too carries the 71B Swanage shed plate.

'Manor Class' No.7828 *Odney Manor* at Minehead on the West Somerset Railway. Although *Odney Manor* is undoubtedly a Great Western locomotive, largely built to Charles Collett's 1938 design, it was in fact built in December 1950 at Swindon by British Railways after nationalisation. Shed 84J was located at Croes Newydd near Wrexham in North Wales. When it first entered service, the locomotive would have carried shed plate 84G for Shrewsbury.

British Railways Standard Class 9F, No.92203 *Black Prince* at Sheringham on the North Norfolk Railway. 85B was the code for one of the Gloucester sheds.

Obviously, with streamlined designs, the splashers were hidden beneath the casing.

In addition to a nameplate if appropriate, numberplates either side of the cab and on the smokebox door, and a maker's plate usually somewhere on the boiler and the tender – which would also have its own number – there would also be a shed plate with a number identifying the locomotive's 'home' shed, fixed to the bottom of the smokebox door. That could mean as many as eight separate individually cast-iron plates on a GWR tender locomotive – a hugely labour-intensive undertaking multiplied by the many thousands of locomotives across Britain's hundreds of early railway companies. In later years, most railway companies – the GWR remained an exception – painted on the cabside numbers, reducing the total to six.

Some companies stopped naming their locomotives quite early on, just giving them numbers, reducing the required number of cast metal plates.

The most prolific 'namers' were the London & North Western Railway and the Great Western, while at the other end of the scale, the Lancashire & Yorkshire named virtually none. The L&NWR nameplate was unique, and remained consistent in its design from 1847 until the railway was

above: A mixture of serif and sans-serif lettering on the enamelled cast brass number plate of Hunslet No. 1430, built in 1922 for the narrow-auge railway from Padern to the harbour at Port Dinorwic, Gwynedd.

above right: The maker's plate on a locomotive built in Newton-le-Willows originally for Indian Railways in 1911, but later transferred to Pakistan Railways. It is now displayed in the Science Museum in Manchester.

0-6-0WT *Bellerophon* displaying the Crewe Heritage Centre cast head board during a visit some years ago. The locomotive was built at Haydock Foundry in 1874 and spent much of its early working life on the Lancashire & Yorkshire Railway. It is owned by the Vintage Carriages Trust at Ingrow in Yorkshire, and until its boiler certificate expired in 2018, was regularly steamed on the Keighley & Worth Valley Railway. It is known as a 'well-tank' locomotive as the water tank is positioned low down under the boiler between the frames.

absorbed into the London, Midland & Scottish. It combined nameplate and maker's plate in one elegant curved piece of cast brass – see Crewe-built Hardwicke's plate on page 95.

After grouping in 1927, a pattern emerged with all the 'Big Four' companies, of naming their new express engines, sometimes reviving names which could be traced back to the railways' earliest days.

left: A steam locomotive was constructed from from hundreds of often-complex castings hundreds of castings, large and small, but special care was given to the numberplate – and nameplate if there was one. No.1054, built at Crewe in 1881, is the last operational locomotive of the London & North Western Railway.

below: A combination of moulds and photographs gives a sense of the scale of the Great Western Railway's casting shed – a display in the STEAM Museum in the former GWR Swindon Works. 'Green's Emergency Cupola', built in Keighley from 1900, was used when relatively small quantities of iron or brass were required for a casting.

above: The cast brass nameplate on *Gazelle*, the smallest preserved standard-gauge locomotive in Britain, built in 1893 by A. Dodman & Co Ltd., Highgate Works, Kings Lynn, a private order for a Mr William Burkett. It is now displayed in the Colonel Stephens Museum at Tenterden.

top right: GWR No.6000 *King George V* at the Steam Museum in Swindon, displaying 'The Bristolian' cast-metal headboard and shed plate 82C for Swindon.

above: The cast-metal nameplate on 'new build' Peppercorn Pacific *Tornado* – which first steamed 58 years after its designer, Arthur Peppercorn's early death in 1951 – with the addition of the painted crest of RAF Leeming, where the RAF's Tornado F3s were stationed until withdrawn in 2008.

Shed codes were first introduced around 1907, quite late in railway history, when the Midland adopted a policy of fixing small circular plates carrying the shed number to the foot of each locomotive's smokebox door.

The shed codes we recognise today, however, did not appear until the 1930s, and were based on an initiative from the LMS which was later modified after nationalisation when British Railways standardised the size and typographic style of the plates.

Each railway company had previously had its own system of shed identification. The GWR, for example gave each depot a code of two to five letters based on tits location, and in addition each shed had a two- or three-digit number. Thus the code for Worcester – which had been WOS 215 in GWR days, became Shed 85A under British Railways.

There could be as many as eight separate individually cast-iron plates on a GWR tender locomotive, for example – a hugely labour-intensive undertaking multiplied by the many thousands of locomotives across Britain's hundreds of early railway companies. In later years, most railway companies – the GWR remained an exception – painted on the cabside numbers, reducing the total to six.

As work patterns changed – especially after nationalisation – locomotives could be assigned to several different sheds in the course of their working life, so nterchangeability was essential. The standardised cast-metal shed plates which was introduced across the entire railway network measured 4.5 x 7.5 inches –120mm x 190mm – thus enabling a simple change of plate to be implemented whenever a locomotive was assigned to a different shed.

In addition to all the different signage on locomotives, most freight wagons had a numberplate identifying the railway company to which they belonged, its inventory number, and often additional information on where and when it had been made.

A considerable proportion of freight vehicles pre-nationalisation, however, were privately owned, and thus did not appear anywhere on the railway companies' stock lists. They were usually identified only by their owners' names painted on the sides.

Just when such plates started to be used is uncertain, but it was certainly long before grouping that first attempts to standardise the shape and size of these plates appear to have been made.

What emerged was what became known as the 'D Plate' and, usually made in cast-iron, they were produced in their millions. The pattern for the sign would be entirely assembled in wood in the pattern shop before being used twice to create two plates per wagon.

Pre-nationalisation, the Midland, GWR, LNER, LMS and Southern all finished their plates to a high quality, while the British Railways approach

above left: A broken cast-iron GWR private owner's wagon plate from 1908 displayed in the Museum of the Cholsey & Wallingford Railway at Wallingford, Oxfordshire.

above: The nameplate and maker's plate on the Ffestiniog & Welsh Highland Railway's 1971-built *Trangkil No.4*, the most recent narrow-gauge steam locomotive to be built by The Hunslett Engine Co. Ltd. of Leeds.

below left: Maker's plate from 1919-built GCR 'Large Director Class' No.506 *Butler Henderson*. It had cost £7,620 to build.

below: Charles Roberts & Co. Ltd. was a major manufacturer of railway wagons, established in 1856, moving to Horbury, a suburb of Wakefield in 1873. Through a series of mergers, the company became part of Bombardier, before closing in 2005.

above: One of the few surviving Simplex 4wDM shunting locomotives, this example was built by the Motor Rail & Tramcar Company of Bedford in 1919 and was destined for War Department use. It originally had a Dorman petrol engine, but this was replaced by a Lister diesel by the present owner. It now carries the name *Ubique* on the frame. The many cast-metal plates attached to the engine cowling (*below right*) are a visual history of the locomotive. Shed plate 21G is the shed number for the Chasewater Railway in Staffordshire where it is currently based.

seems to have been somewhat more utilitarian – but then, the sheer scale of the re-equipping necessary in the immediate post-nationalisation years, as Britain recovered from the Second World War, was immense.

Examples of 'D plates' from early railway companies, as well as those produced by or for British Railways are now highly collectible – so much so, in fact, the replica LNER and LMS plates are widely available online.

When one considers just how many railway companies there initially were, and how many locomotive and rolling stock builders supplied them, the number of cast-metal plates and signs which must have been cast is astronomical.

But just as important as the cast signage on locomotives and rolling stock was the proliferation of signage in stations and along the trackside.

From James Charles Inglis's *Engineering Department Instructions* manual published by the GWR's Swindon Works in 1898, it is clear that, by that time, the more widely used signs were readily available 'off the shelf', while less common ones were 'made to order'. Inglis had been appointed the Chief Engineer six years earlier in 1892. The manual, (*see pages 108-109*) was part of his drive to standardise procedures across the company's entire network, thus reinforcing the GWR's brand identity. It makes clear that there already were established design protocols, dictating type size and layout but it is clear from surviving examples that, despite it commendable intentions, the the design conventions laid down in its pages were not always followed.

This remarkable document also makes it clear that, even before the end of the 19th century, each GWR. station was considered a separate cost

above: The Motor Rail & Tramcar Company's maker's plate on *Ubique*. The company used this name and logo from 1911 until 1931.

RAILWAY SIGNAGE – NAMES, NUMBERS AND INSTRUCTIONS

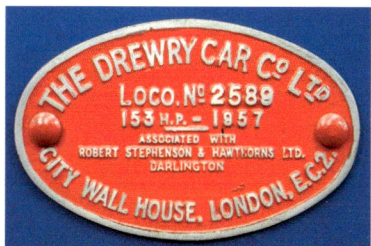

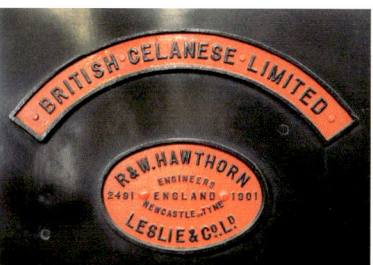

top left: The Drewry Car Co designed diesel shunters, but sub-contracted their construction. This example, built for Dover Gasworks, is preserved at Barrow Hill.

left: Cast metal head board on the Ffestiniog Railway's *Prince*, built in 1863.

far left: British Celanese was the first chemical company to manufactuer isopropyl alcohol. later becoming part of Courtaulds.

below: Maker's plate on a Sheffield-built class 02 shunter, preserved in Barrow Hill Roundhouse.

left: The interior of the Midand Railway's Barrow Hill Roundhouse near Chesterfield, the last operational roundhouse left on the British railway network. Its 24-road internal layout can still be accessed by the original 1931 turntable. It is now home to a collection of heritage steam locomotives and preserved diesels.

bottom: Cowans Sheldon & Company's maker's plate on the turntable in the centre of the Barrow Hill roundhouse. The Carlisle-based heavy engineering company was a major manufacturer of turntables, travelling railway cranes and other heavy equipment, and once one of the city's major employers.

centre, working to a strict devolved budget – if the Station Master needed to replace a sign, he had to buy a new one from the stores department at Swindon (*see the price lists on pages 108-109*). Thus, the onus was clearly on him to ensure that his staff maintained every aspect of the fabric, including the signage, to ensure longevity and reduce costs.

The penalties for breaking rules, or for causing even accidental damage which might result in repair costs, were severe, resulting in deductions from already-meagre wages. Transgressions would be recorded in a fines book maintained by each station master. Around the time the GWR book was published, the railway was transitioning from wooden signage to cast metal in stations, in sheds, and along the permanent way, and the manual required that, if necessary, all wooden signage be replaced

above: Outdoor points levers at Norden Station on the Swanage Railway, each with its cast metal plaque. Approaching the station is former Southern Railway 'U Class' Mogul No.31806.

above right & far right: Water capacity plates were also cast in iron – and sometimes brass. A GWR 'King Class' tender carried 4,000 gallons, while 2-6-0 *City of Truro*'s tender, carried 3,000,

right: British Railways Brighton-built standard class 4MT 2-6-4 from 1955 carried 2,000 gallons,

by cast-iron, as and when a station was being refurbished or repainted. It defined the sizes of lettering for each specific purpose.

While many of the principles and processes involved in creating the infra-structure for a railway were described in the sort of detail one would expect, there are no instructions laid down for the manufacture of all the hundreds of signs which were cast in the Swindon Works.

The same lack of instruction is true of many other foundry and workshop manuals consulted in the course of the research for this book – a surprising omission as the skills of the pattern-maker and the foundryman were by no means easily learned. The signs, however, offer a fascinating insight into social history. For example, with a labourer only earning about 15 shillings a week, and a skilled artisan 30 shillings, a 'forty

left: The cast nameplate from Old Oak Common signal box is now preserved at Didcot Railway Centre.

below left: Tyer's Electric Train Tablet system – a key piece of signal-box equipment, designed for single track lines – with the company's enamelled cast brass plaque on the front. Inserting the tablet in the slot at the bottom locked the signals and ensured a train had exclusive access to a section of the line. This example is preserved in the Colonel Stephens Museum at Tenterden Town Station on the Kent & East Sussex Railway.

below: Cranmore Signal Box on the East Somerset Railway has two cast-iron signs – one carrying its name and the other 'Beware of Trains'. Unseen here, the author is driving the locomotive. (photo: Kath Hannavy)

following pages: The 1898 GWR book *Engineering Department Instructions* includes a price list for 'off-the-shelf' cast-iron signs and individual letters.

Cast Iron Letters, &c.

Cast iron letters, &c., kept in stock.

535. The following is a list of cast iron letters, plates and figures kept in stock at Swindon, (see also paragraph No. 352):—

Reference No.	Size.		Description.	Price each.
	in.	in.		
A 1	8 ×	4½	"In"	3d.
2	,,		"Out"	3d.
B 1	16 ×	2½	"Tickets" ...	3d.
C 1	18 ×	3½	"Inspectors" ...	6d.
2	,,		"Porters"	6d.
3	,,		"Guards"	6d.
4	,,		"Stores"	6d.
5	,,		"Private"	6d.
6	,,		"Gentlemen" ...	6d.
7	,,		"Lavatory" ...	6d.
D 1	19 ×	8	"Ladies' Room, 1st and 2nd Class"	1/3
2	,,		"Ladies Room, 3rd Class"	1/3
3	,,		"Waiting Room, 1st and 2nd Class"	1/3
	,,		"Waiting Room, 3rd Class"	1/3
	,,		"Parcels and Cloak Room"	1/3
E 1	24 ×	3½	"Lamp Room" ...	8d.
2	,,		"Waiting Room" ...	8d.
3	,,		"Booking Office" ...	8d.
4	,,		"Station Master" ...	8d.
5	,,		"Ticket Collector"	8d.
6	,,		"Ladies' Room" ...	8d.
7	,,		"Parcel Office" ...	8d.
8	,,		"Cloak Room" ...	8d.

179

Cast Iron Letters, &c.—*continued*.

Reference No.	Size.	Description.	Price each.
	in. in.		
F 1	15 × 9	"The issue of Tickets, &c."	1/-
2	,,	"Please adjust your dress, &c."	1/-
3	,,	"No admission except, &c."	1/-
G 1	23½ × 12	"All persons found trespassing, &c."	2/-
2	30 × 21	Trespass Notice ...	4/-
3	34 × 24	Explosives Act Notice	5/-
4	30½ × 16½	Locomotive Act Notice	4/-
5	31 × 9¾	Level Crossing Gate Notice	2/6
6	43½ × 18½	"Passengers are requested to cross the line by the Bridge"	8/-
7	43½ × 18½	"Passengers are requested to cross the line by Subway"	8/-
	1 in.	Letters A to Z, &, and Figures 0, 1 to 9	4½d. doz.
	1½ ,,	Do. do.	5d. ,,
	2 ,,	Do. do.	5½d. ,,
	2½ ,,	Do. do.	6d. ,,
	3 ,,	Do. do.	7d. ,,
	4 ,,	Do. do.	8d. ,,
	5 ,,	Do. do.	1/- ,,
	6 ,,	Do. do.	1/3 ,,
	7 ,,	Do. do.	1/9 ,,
	9 ,,	Do. do.	2/9 ,,
	12 ,,	Do. do.	3/6 ,,
	18 ,,	Do. do.	16/3 ,,

clockwise from top; Oliver Bulleid's 1941-built 'Merchant Navy Class' locomotive *Canadian Pacific*, built for the Southern Railway, carries several cast-metal plates, including the 'Atlantic Coast Express' header board.

The numberplate and maker's plate on the former South African Railway's 'Class 15F' 4-8-2 No.3007, now displayed in Glasgow's Riverside Museum at Pointhouse.

The original cast numberplate from the John Aspinall-designed L&YR 0-6-0 locomotive No.1300. Currently carrying BR No. 52322, it is based on the East Lancashire Railway.

Sitting on the splasher behind the locomotive's leaf springs, *City of Truro*'s enamelled brass nameplate. The 1903-built 4-4-0 GWR '3700 Class' locomotive is said by some sources to have been the first to exceed 100mph, on a run between Plymouth and London Paddington.

The brass numberplate on 1925-built GWR 0-6-2T No.5637, now based on the East Somerset Railway.

Andrew Barclay's 1920-built 0-4-0ST locomotive *Lady Nan*, Works No 1719, also now based at Cranmore on the East Somerset Railway.

The number and maker's plate on the the 1886-built Caledonian Railway No.123, built by Neilson in Glasgow. In 1914 it was put into reserve and re-numbered as 1123, later given an LMS number 1400. The locomotive is now on static display in the Riverside Museum in Glasgow.

Maker's plate manufactured at Didcot Railway Centre in 2018.

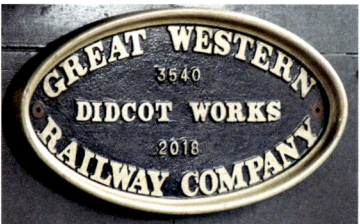

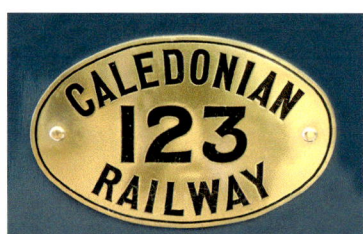

shillings' fine in 1845, *opposite*, was truly punitive. By 1885 the cumulative effects of inflation meant that that amount had about half the buying power. By 1906 – *see the S&DJR sign on p113* – the average working man's weekly wage had risen to 30 shillings (£1.50). Imagine a fine today of about £2,000 for failing to shut a gate, and the 'fear factor' of such a threat is obvious.

Clearly, however, the cost of updating the penalties, and replacing the signs, to keep pace with inflation was not considered to be a worthwhile investment for the railway companies.

The forty shillings fine was the maximum permitted by law, so such signage appeared across almost all of the many companies which used the network. In the case of the Somerset and Dorset, their signs were identical to those of the London & South Western Railway's – which was joint owner of the line with the Midland Railway, and in whose workshops all the S&D signs were cast. Only the company name was changed from the patterns used for casting L&SWR signage.

above: In 1898, if a replacement sign like this was needed, it would have cost the station master about eightpence (3p) out of his devoted budget.

left & far left: Two signs from Hadlow Road Station in Willaston on the Wirral. In a piece of Victorian bureaucratic excess, each company insisted on a version of the sign with its name first. *(Images: R. M Callender)*

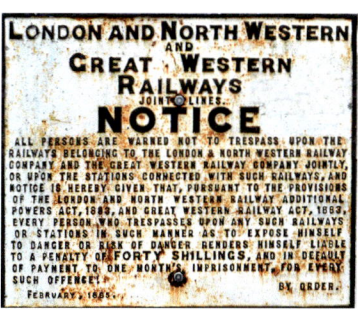

clockwise from below left: The maker's bottom plate on a South African Railways, 1930-built, Beyer-Garrett 4-8-2+2-8-4 locomotive No.2352, built in Gorton, Manchester, by Beyer Peacock & Company Ltd. The locomotive is now in Manchester's Science Museum.

Three of the numerous plates on a tanker wagon, which was originally used to transport Pratt's Perfection Spirit. In 1912 it was registered with the Furness Railway Company –, 'F. Rly. Co'. Hurst, Nelson & Co Ltd, were major manufacturers of both railway rolling stock and tramcars. The tanker is now at Didcot Railway Centre.

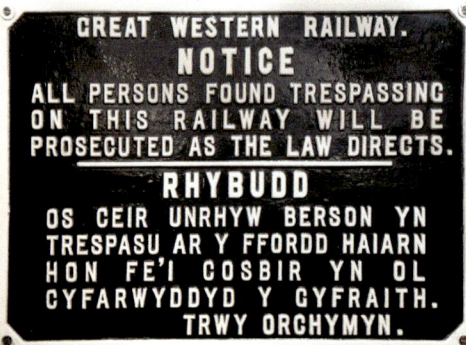 

Five GWR notices from 1845-1932. A consistent corporate style was never fully adopted for its trackside signage.

top left: An interesting use of different type sizes to emphasis and help convey an important message.

top right: A stylised hand adds emphasis.

middle left: Dual language signage was used on the Rhymney, the London & North Western and the Great Western railways.

middle right: A grammatical oddity, the GWR signmakers used 'Company' as a plural rather than a singular noun, using 'give' rather than 'gives'.

right: A fine of forty shillings was a huge amount in 1845 when the average weekly wage was a quarter of that. '8 Vic.Cap.20.S.75' refers to the 1845 *Railway Clauses Consolidation Act*.

On English and Welsh lines, the forty shilling fine was applied to 'trespass' signs used to dissuade the public from accessing railway property. The very limited laws of trespass in Scotland meant that such signs were very rarely erected.

Cost, however, does not seem to have been a barrier to unnecessary duplication, on lines where control was shared between two railway companies. On the Wirral Line in Cheshire, where the Great Western and the London and North Western jointly shared management and usage, each company apparently required signs which gave them apparent primacy.

The Great Western and the London and North Western both had the additional consideration on several of their lines into Wales, that the growing movement, even in the 1880s, to promote the use of the Welsh language, had to be accommodated. While simple messages could be

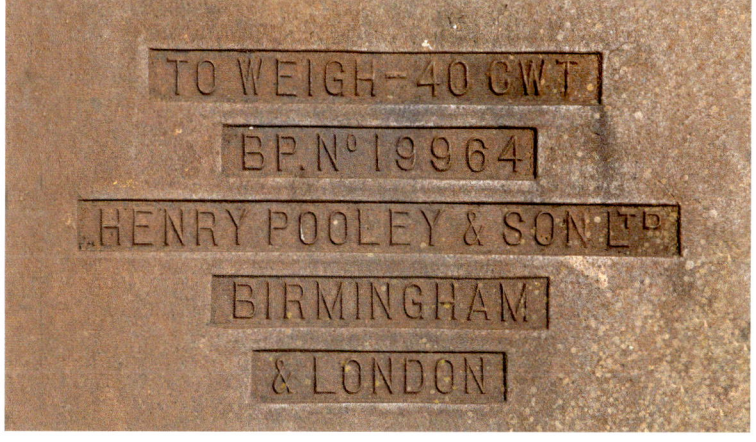

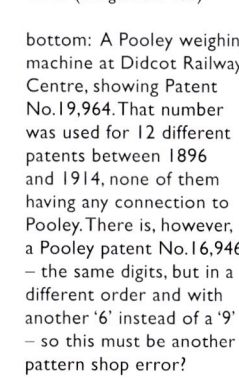

far left: Pooley patent platform weighing machine, at Haverthwaite Station, on the Lakeside & Haverthwaite Railway, Cumbria. It was probably acquired new in the early years of the Furness Railway branch line, and manufactured by Henry Pooley & Son of Liverpool some time before 1896. The Pooleys were prolific 'improvers' of cast-iron weighing machines, taking out numerous patents between 1847 and 1924 – this design was patented in 1847. For decades, the company had a virtual monopoly in station weighing machines, many of which survive today, all over the world.

above left: In 1896, after the move to Kidsgrove, the legend 'Patentees Liverpool' below the royal coat of arms, was replaced by 'Birmingham and London'. This example is on Great Malvern Station which had opened 36 years earlier.

left: Cast-iron weighing bed of a Pooley luggage weighing machine, on the platform of Deal Station in Kent. The post, topped by its rocking steel-yard weighing bar, would have sat on the round plate at the back. The cited patent – No.19431 – does not exist. (*image: Paul Fox*)

bottom: A Pooley weighing machine at Didcot Railway Centre, showing Patent No.19,964. That number was used for 12 different patents between 1896 and 1914, none of them having any connection to Pooley. There is, however, a Pooley patent No.16,946 – the same digits, but in a different order and with another '6' instead of a '9' – so this must be another pattern shop error?

above: The cast-iron maker's plate from the front of Pooley's' 'Automatic Indicator Weighing Machine' based on their 1908 Patent No.20,067.

below: Replica Southern Railway sign are available on the internet.

bottom: Well preserved Somerset and Dorset Railway trespass sign, now displayed in Radstock Museum, Somerset. Radstock was served by both the S&DR and GWR. In 1906, when this sign was created, Godfrey Knight was the secretary of the London & South Western Railway and William Clower was secretary of the Midland Railway, the S&D's joint owners.

displayed in both languages on a single sign, *(ee page 112)*, notices with more wordage required two separate signs.

One thing which remarkable about the proliferation of signage is the quality control which must have been exercised over their production. Given the tens of thousands of different signs produced for the railways alone, spelling mistakes, or other errors, are virtually unknown – but some quite surprising ones have been identified.

Henry Pooley & Son Ltd., of the Albion Works in Liverpool, was one of the market leaders in railway and dockside weighing equpiment. The initial development of the weighing machines in the early 1830s was down to the 'Son' of H. Pooley & Son – also named Henry – responding to the need for cargo weighing machines on the recently-opened Liverpool & Manchester Railway. His first weighing machines patent was dated 1847.

From the 1890s, initially led by the third Henry Pooley to head the company – the grandson of the founder – took out more than 50 patents to protect the company's designs, asserting the company's cast-iron patent credentials on each machine.

Some of those weighing machines were supplied on wheels so they could be moved around platforms or quaysides, others were set into the platform itself. They were available in a wide range of sizes and weight capacities, and usually carried the company's name, product number, and Liverpool & London.

The large recessed cast-iron weighing machine platform on Deal Station, *(see page 113)*, carries the legend 'H. Pooley & Son Ltd Birmingham & London BP No.19431' – the company had moved in 1896 to the Union Foundry in Kidsgrove – renamed the Albion Foundry, as in Liverpool – and had moved their headquarters to Birmingham.

However, there is no British Patent No.19431 in Pooley's name, but there is a Patent No.13491 – the same numbers in reverse order – the application dated 13 July 1896 and the complete specification accepted 4 July 1896; and that was for a weighing machine employing the same basic principles found in all three of the examples illustrated on page 113. The platform plate on the example at Didcot Railway Centre carries patent numberNo.19,964 – but that does not relate to any Pooley patent.

In the absence of an alternate explanation, the conclusion must surely be that patternmakers occasionally assembled the individual wooden letters on to the wooden patternbase in the wrong order, and their supervisors did not check carefully enough before the sand mould was made and the plate cast.

RAILWAY SIGNAGE – NAMES, NUMBERS AND INSTRUCTIONS

top left: Cast-aluminium plate added to former BR shunter 08 123. named after one of early benefactors of the Cholsey & Wallingford Railway in Oxfordshire. Between 1952 and 1962, 996 '08s' were built.

top right: Even the lavatory drain cock on BR Mark I coaches had its own cast-metal sign.

middle: Logo of the Great Northern Railway on a the former Handyside Bridge – also known as the 'Harry Potter Bridge' from King's Cross Station, now preserved at Ropley. on the Mid-Hants Railway. The cast- and wrought-iron bridge dates from 1893, years after King's Cross station first opened. It was built by Andrew Handyside & Company of Derby, creators of a vast amount of our surviving cast-iron Victorian architecture,.

left: Catch Points sign at Barrow Hill sidings. Catch points are used to divert, and sometimes derail, runaway vehicles experiencing brake failure, or which are otherwise out of control.

top left. Chain-driven 0-4-0 Sentinel vertical-boilered, steam shunter, built at the Sentinel Waggon Works in Shrewsbury, 1926, and operated by the GWR, then the LMS, and later BR. Its drive system was covered by 1924 British Patent No.248835. It is currently at the Cholsey & Wallingford Railway.

top right: 'Patent Sentinel Locomotive' cast-metal axle-box cover on one of the Sentinel's wheels.

right: A 1961-built, Rolls-Royce-powered Sentinel diesel. The maker's name is incorporated into the cast-metal headlamp surround...

below right: ...and also displayed on the cab sides.

below far right: The axle box covers from the Sentinel diesel.

bottom: The name *Pendennis Castle* was originally carried by GWR 'Castle Class' steam locomotive No.4079 which was sold to Australia in 1977. The name was re-assigned to rebuilt Class 47 diesel, re-numbered as Class 57, No.57604. Since, the original 4079 was returned to Britain and restored, two locos now carry the same name.

top left: Pausing for a photo-stop at the entrance to the half-mile Mirandol Tunnel on the 'Chemin de Fer Touristique du Haut Quercy' which runs from Martel to St. Denis-les-Martel in the Dordogne, the 1927-built side tank (040 T-class) 0-8-0T locomotive No.7477, was built by the Société Alsacienne de Constructions Mechanique (known as SACM) in Illkirch-Graffenstaden, a suburb of Strasbourg.

upper inset: Locomotive No.7477"s maker's plate.

lower inset: The maker's plate from the locomotive, *Trambouze*, an 0-6-0T built by Schneider et Cie at Le Creuzot in eastern France in 1891.

right: *Trambouze* and the sheds at Martel station on the heritage railway, 'Le Truffadou', built to carry timber for making wine casks, and the truffles for which the Martel area was famous throughout France.

below: Cast-iron maker's plate on the adjustable counterbalance of a 6,000 kilogram capacity travelling crane built for the 'Société Générale des Chemins de Fer Économiques', currently on static display at Martel station.

By the 1920s, 90% of the weighng machines on Britain's railways were Pooley's, and to service and calibrate them, they even had their own wagons and mobile workshops to transport engineers and equipment around the country – by rail, of course.

Today, cast-metal signage on the railways is in decline, being replaced by plastic and other materials.

The beautifully-finished cast-metal nameplates on locomotives, however, continue the tradition started nearly two centuries ago.

SITES & COLLECTIONS FEATURED IN THIS BOOK

Barrow Hill Roundhouse Railway Centre
www.barrowhill.org   tel: 01246 280077
Campbell Drive, Barrow Hill, Chesterfield S43 2PR
Home of Britain's last operational roundhouse with its collection of heritage locomotives built by the Midland Railway in 1870. The current turntable, by Cowans Sheldon of Carlisle, dates from 1931 and is regularly demonstrated. Also on site is the former Pinxton Signal Box. Admission charge.

Beamish: The Living Museum of the North
www.beamish.org.uk   tel: 0191 370 4000
Beamish, County Durham, DH9 0RG
Huge open air museum includes recreated Victorian town with shops, railway, trams, Beamish Colliery engine house and pit yard. The 1855 colliery winding engine is steamed daily. Drift mine tour. Demonstrations of Victorian crafts includes such things as bread and cake making and making boiled sweets feature regularly. There is also an opportunity to see how a small local newspaper was printed. Check website for events. Admission charge.

Big Pit: National Coal Museum Wales
www.museumwales.ac.uk/en/bigpit   tel: 029 2057 3650
Blaenafon, Torfaen, NP4 9XP
Part of the Blaenafon World Heritage Site. Preserved mine with underground tours. Extensive site includes a recreation of a coal face with cutting equipment. Superb museum in miners' bathhouse tells the story of the South Wales coalfields. Admission free, but a charge for the car park

Blaenavon Ironworks
cadw.wales.gov.uk/daysout/blaenavonironworks   tel: 01495 792615
North Street, Blaenavon, NP4 9RN
Extensive remains of late 18th century ironworks, expanded and developed in the 19th century. In 2000 Blaenavon was awarded World Heritage Site status for the industrial landscape including the Ironworks and the nearby Big Pit. The ironworks site includes furnaces, the impressive Balance Tower, workers cottages and a recreation of the company's shop. Open daily, admission free.

left: *'Elsie'* is a 1902-built 180hp tandem compound steam engine, buit by J. W. McNaught & Company of Rochdale for Rochdale's Barchant Spinning Company. Now preserved in Bolton Steam Museum, the engine is known today as the 'Wasp Mill Engine' after its move to Wasp Mill in Wardle, near Rochdale, in 1917 where it worked fo the next 50 years.

Bolton SteamMuseum
www.nmes.org   tel: 01204 846490
Mornington Road, Bolton BL1 4EU
Home to the Northern Mill Engine Society Collection, Bolton Steam Museum is housed in a large former warehouse at the Musgrave Spinning Company's Atlas Mills – once one of the largest spinning complexes in the country. The collection has grown steadily over the past 50 years and now comprises more than 30 engines. There are 5 steaming weekends each year, but the engines can be viewed, some turned by electricity, every Wednesday and Sunday – check website for dates and details. Admission free, but donations appreciated.

Bristol Floating Harbour
www.bristolfloatingharbour.org.uk   tel: 0117 903 1484
Welsh Back, Bristol BS1 4SPU
Created by William Jessop and modified by Isambard Kingdom Brunel and others, the harbour is home to the only surviving example in Britain of a Fairbairn steam crane – built in Bath by Stothert & Pitt whose own design of crane line the harbourside – and a collection of unique vessels.

British Motor Museum
www.britishmotormuseum.co.uk tel: 01926 895300
Banbury Road, Gaydon, Warwickshire, CV35 0BJ
The museum's 'Time Road' is an innovative way of explaining how, as vehicles developed, the roads on which they ran were also improved – from the dust and rubble roads of the Victorian era to the smoother surfaces of today. The cars displayed along the 'Time Road' stand on surfaces which are typical of the time when they were built. Admission charge.

Burrington Churchyard
Burrington, Herefordshire, SY8 2HT
The churchyard at St. George's church is home to eight very rare cast-iron grave slabs, cast locally, some dating from the first quarter of the 17th century

Bursledon Brickworks
www.bursledonbrickworks.org.uk tel: 01489 576248
Swanwick Lane, Swanwick, Southampton, SO31 7HB
A rare time capsule, the brickworks were never updated and when they closed, the men were still cutting and working the clay in the same manner as had their Victorian and Edwardian forefathers. The museum has practical demonstrations of brickmaking using original steam-powered machinery. Open daily. Admission charge.

Caen Hill Locks, Devizes
www.canalandrivertrust.org.uk   tel: 01452 318000
Caen Hill, Devizes, SN10 1RF
John Rennie's amazing flight of locks and lagoons on the Kennet and Avon Canal climbing the steep hill up to Devizes. Access available at all times.

Cholsey & Wallingford Railway
www.cholsey-wallingford-railway.com   tel: 01491 835067

SITES & COLLECTIONS FEATURED IN THIS BOOK

Wallingford Station, 5 Hithercroft Road, Wallingford, Oxfordshire, OX10 9G
Preserved GWR branch line. Wallingford Station now has the former platform canopy from Maidenhead station. The railway mainly operates diesels, including, at the time of writing, several Class 08 shunters and a Linwood-built single-coach diesel 'bubble-car' built by the Pressed Steel company in. 1961. A rare chain-driven Sentinel Class Y1 shunter, formerly of the LNER, awaits overhaul.

Claverton Pumping Station
www.claverton.org   tel: 01225 483001
Ferry Lane, Claverton, Bath, BA2 7BH
Restored 1813 Water-powered pumping station designed by John Rennie, built to raise water from the River Avon up to the Kennet and Avon Canal. Check website for operating days. Admission charge.

Coalbrookdale
www.ironbridge.org.uk/our-attractions   tel: 01952 435900
Coalbrookdale, Shropshire, TF8 5UD
In addition to the Iron Bridge itself, there are ten Ironbridge Gorge Museums, including Blists Hill Victorian Town. Admission charges.

Colonel Stephens Museum, Kent & East Sussex Railway
www.kesr.org.uk tel: 01580 765155
Tenterden Town Station, Station Rd, Tenterden, Kent TN30 6HE
The line follows part of the Rother Valley Railway opened in 1899. Colonel Stephens was involved and was, for a time, a director. It closed to passengers in 1961. It now operates over 11.5 miles of track between Tenterden Town and Bodiam. The Colonel Stephens Railway Museum is opposite Tenterden Town Station. Admission charge.

Didcot Railway Centre
www.didcotrailwaycentre.org.uk tel: 01235 817200
Didcot, Oxfordshire OX11 7NJ
Huge collection of GWR locomotives, rolling stock and ephemera. The Didcot collection is said to be the largest collection representing a single company anywhere in the world. Standard gauge and broad gauge. Admission charge.

East Somerset Railway
www.eastsomersetrailway.com tel: 01749 880417
Cranmore Station, West Cranmore, Shepton Mallet, Somerset BA4 4QP
The 2.5-mile line from Cranmore to Mendip Vale was re-opened by the artist David Shepherd in 1974. Cranmore Station's buildings were rescued from both Wells and Westbury-sub-Mendip.

Fakentam Town Gasworks
www.fakenhamgasmuseum.com tel: 01553 762151
Hempton Road, Fakenham, NR21 7LA
The gasworks produced town gas from 1846 to 1965. After closure it was preserved and is the only one remaining in England. The collections include displays of lighting, heating, cooking and domestic equipment, gas street lamps, water heaters, cookers, stoves, fires, domestic gas lighting and gas meters. Open Thursday, Friday and Bank Holidays. Admission free.

Frogmore Paper Mill
www.thepapertrail.org.uk tel: 01442 234600
Fourdrinier Way, Hemel Hempstead, Hertfordshire HP3 9R
The world's oldest mechanised paper mill – the birthplace of paper's industrial revolution. It is still a working paper mill producing around 100 tonnes of specialist grade paper every year on historic paper machines. Guided tours and a hands-on opportunity to make paper in the traditional way. Admission charge.

Gayle Mill
www.thepapertrail.org.uk tel: 01969 6293480
Gayle Lane, Hawes DL8 3RZ
Believed to be the oldest structurally unaltered cotton mill in existence, the late 18th century mill still contains its early vortex water turbine by Williamson Brothers of Kendal. Admission charge.

Highlands End Holiday Park
www.wdlh.co.uk tel: 0117 903 1484
Eype, Bridport DT6 6AR
Home to a collection of historic fire engines, Victorian fire insurance plaques and fire brigade memorabilia, including Bridport Museum's rare 1902 horse-drawn Merryweather steam engine on long-term loan.

Lakeside & Haverthwaite Railway
www.lakesiderailway.co.uk tel: 01539 531594
Haverthwaite Station, nr Ulverston, Cumbria LA12 8AL
The former Furness Railway branchline to Lakeside, opened in 1869 and axed by BR in 1965, was re-opened on 2 May by Bishop, and eminent railway photographer, Eric Treacy. Steam trains run 3.5 miles between Haverthwaite and Lakeside and connect with the steamer services on Lake Windermere.

Museum of Science & Industry, Manchester
www.mosi.org.uk tel: 0161 832 2244
Liverpool Road, Castlefield, Manchester, M3 4FP
Housed in five listed buildings including Liverpool Road Station, the world's first passenger station, the museum covers a wide range of themes focusing on Manchester's contribution to science and industry. The six sections of the Revolution Manchester gallery explore Transport Revolutions, Computer Age, Engineering, Energy, Cottonopolis and the Structure of Matter.

Mid-Hants Railway (The Watercress Line)
www.watercressline.co.uk tel: 01962 733810
Station Road, Alresford, Hampshire SO24 9JG
The Watercress Line runs for 10 miles from New Alresford to Alton. Steam services run most weekends, and daily in summer. Large roster of locomotives from Southern Railways, LMS and BR Southern Region.

National Museum of the Royal Navy
www.nmrn.org.uk/our-museums/national-museum-royal-navy-hartlepool   tel: 01429 860077
Maritime Ave, Hartlepool, Cleveland TS24 0XZ
Formerly known as the Hartlepool Maritime Experience, this is effectively three museums on the same

site – Hartlepool Maritime Museum, the 1817 Mumbai-built HMS *Trincomalee* and former Humber ferry PS *Wingfield Castle* built In Hartlepool in 1934. The recreated quayside contains the type of shops which would have been found near most 18th and 19th century docks. Admission charge.

National Railway Museum
www.railwaymuseum.org.uk tel: 0330 058 0058
Leeman Rd, York YO26 4XJ
Home to a vast collection of locomotives, rolling stock, railway ephemera, and extensive archives.

National Slate Museum Wales
www.museumwales.ac.uk/slate tel: 0300 111 2333
Llanberis, Gwynedd, LL55 4TY
Set in the Victorian workshops of Dinorwig Quarry which closed in 1969, the museum tells the story of Welsh slate against the backdrop of Elidir Mountain and its centuries of slate workings. Regular demonstrations of slate dressing and slate carving. The workshops, buildings and surrounding landscape are set out as if workmen have just left for home. Open daily (except Saturdays in winter). Admission free

National Waterways Museum
www. canalrivertrust.org.uk/national-waterways-museum tel: 0151 355 5017
South Pier Road, Ellesmere Port, Merseyside CH65 4FW
This vast museum includes Telford's dock complex built under the direction of William Jessop, steam pumping station, warehouses filled with boats. Boat trips available. Admission charge.

Portsmouth Historic Dockyard
www.historicdockyard.co.uk tel: 023 9283 9766
H.M.Naval Base, Main Rd, Portsmouth PO1 3QX
Vessels include Henry VIII's flagship *Mary Rose*, Nelson's flagship HMS *Victory*, HMS *Warrior*, the only surviving iron-hulled 1860 battleship and Gallipoli veteran HMS *Monitor M33 (Minerva)*, built in 1915. Admission charge.

Radstock Museum of Somerset Coalfield Life
www.radstockmuseum.co.uk tel: 01761 437722
Waterloo Road, Radstock, BA3 3EP
Housed in the town's former market hall, an award-winning museum celebrating the history and heritage of the former Somerset Coalfield and the life of a typical Somerset miner and his family. Outside is the former headgear from Kilmersdon Colliery, one of the last Somerset collieries to close. Admission charge.

SS *Great Britain*
www.ssgreatbritain.org   tel: 0117 926 0680
Great Western Dockyard, Gas Ferry Road, Bristol BS1 6TY
Brunel's great 1844 ship, the world's first propeller-driven passenger ship, was rebuilt from the hulk which returned to Bristol in 1979. The project was completed in 2005. Open daily. Admission charge.

SS *Shieldhall*
www.ss-shieldhall.co.uk   tel: 07751 603 190

Berth 29, Southampton Docks SO14 3XD
Built by Lobnitz & Co. at Renfrew on the Clyde in 1955, *Shieldhall* is the largest surviving passenger/cargo steamship in British waters. Still sailing regularly, she is still powered by her original triple-expansion engines. Available for cruises and private hire, and bookings can be arranged through the website.

STEAM! The Museum of the Great Western Railway
www.railwaymuseum.org.uk tel: 0330 058 0058
Leeman Rd, York YO26 4XJ
Housed in part of the former GWR Swindon Works, the museum tells the Great Western's story and contains a huge collection of locomotives, rolling stock and ephemera. Admission charge.

Strathspey Railway
www.strathspeyrailway.co.uk tel: 01479 810725
Aviemore Station, Dalfaber Road, Aviemore, Inverness-shire, PH22 1PY
Steam trains operate along 10 miles of track from Aviemore to Boat of Garten and Broomhill. The line, opened in 1866, was closed to passengers by BR in 1965. Locomotives include Caledonian Railways No.828.

Sumburgh Head
www.sumbrughhead.com tel: 01950 461966
Sumburgh, Shetland ZE3 9JN
Lighthouse, foghorn, compressor room and museum, plus adjacent nature reseave on the southern tip of Shetland's Mainland.

Summerlee Museum of Scottish Industrial Life
www.northlanarkshire.gov.uk/summerlee tel: 01236 638460
Heritage Way, Coatbridge, ML5 1QD
The museum collection, on the site for the former Summerlee Ironworks, includes an 1810 winding engine, a working tramway, and the 1924 winding engine from the former Cardowen Colliery at Shotts.

Swanage Railway
www.swanagerailway.co.uk tel: 01929 425800
Railway Station Approach, Swanage, Dorset BH19 1HB
Running 6 miles from Swanage, past Corfe Castle, to Norden, steam services are hauled by mainline locomotives and operate daily from late March to the end of October, plus special weekends and galas.

The Robey Trust
www.therobeytrust.co.uk tel: 01822 615960
The New Perseverance Iron Works, Parade Business Park, Pixon Lane, Tavistock, PL19 9RQ
Unique collection of engines and ephemera telling the story of Robey's of Lincoln

Tower Bridge Exhibition
www.towerbridge.org.uk tel: 020 7403 3761
Tower Bridge Road, London, SE1 2UP
A chance to explore the iconic bridge and walk across the glass walkway on the upper level. The exhibition

describing how the bridge was built can be found in the south tower and along the upper walkway. Also open are the Victorian engine rooms below the road on the north side of the river, the engines beautifully restored. Open daily. Admission charge.

Trencherfield Mill Engine, Wigan
http://www.wlct.org/wigan/museums-archives/trencherfield tel: 01942 828128
Heritage Way, Wigan WN3 4EF
The largest working triple-expansion mill engine in the world, built by J. & E. Wood of Bolton in 1907 to power a large spinning mill, the engine is still operational in its original engine house. Now fuelled by bio-fuel rather than coal, and with steam raised in a modern boiler. At the time of writing, the engine has not been steamed for some time, awaiting finance to repair engine-house roof.

Westonzoyland Museum of Steam Power & Land Drainage
www.wzlet.org tel: 01278 691595
Hoopers Lane, Westonzoyland. Bridgwater TA7 0LS
Celebrating the role of steam – and later power sources – in draining the Somerset Levels. Star attraction is the 1861 Easton & Amos patent two-cylinder vertical condensing engine which drove the station's centrifugal pump for 90 years until 1951 and is now regularly run on steaming days. More than 30 engines have been rescued from local factories and mills, making the collection one of the largest in the UK. Admission charge.

Westonbirt – The National Arboretum
www.www.forestryengland.uk/westonbirt-the-national-arboretum tel: 0300 067 4890
Forestr England's Westonbirt, The National Arboretum, Tetbury GL8 8QS
Spectacular forest walks open all the year round. Home to a rare collection of Victorian cast-iron plant labels and signs. Admission charge.

Wookey Hole Paper Mill
www.wookey.co.uk tel: 01749 672243
The Mill, High St, Wookey Hole, Wells, Somerset BA5 1BB
A paper mill since the 17th century, visitors can watch the *Vatman* and his assistant, the *Coucher*, making paper in the traditional way and then have a go at making some paper themselves. Open daily. Admission charge.

ACKNOWLEDGEMENTS

This book could not have been created without the help of a great many people and organisations, so the author offers his thanks to the following for their help: John Spear; John Carruthers; Gillian Smith; Duncan Hannavy; Brian Gooding; Peter Dunn; Nicola Coupe; Dr. Paul Fox; Rob Pringle; Dr. Ron Callender; Eileen Gunn; Peter Rance and Roger Orchard at the Great Western Trust, Didcot; Steven Campion at the British Library; Sean Jones, Mark Hackett and Joe Hackett at Jones n Co Cast Metal Designs Ltd, Coventry; Philip Shardlow of Croft Casting Ltd, Whitby; Sarah Dashwood and Angie Leathley at Gayle Mill, Hawes; Helen Chick at Forestry England's Westonbirt National Arboretum, Gloucestershire; Jane Schon and colleagues at the Wiltshire Museum, Devizes; The Science and Industry Museum, Manchester; Martin Cox at Highlands End Holiday Park, Eype, Dorset; Nick Turner and colleagues at Radstock Museum; Alex Masters and colleagues at The Robey Trust in Tavistock; Fakenham Gasworks Museum, Norfolk; Hannah Little at the Clifton Suspension Bridge & Museum.

FURTHER READING

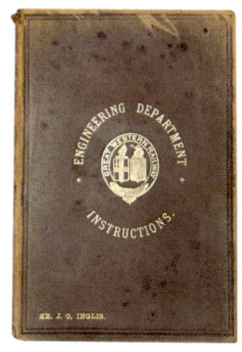

above: The front cover of Inglis's *Engineering Department Instructions* manual, now preserved in the collection of the Great Western Trust at Didcot. See also pp108-109

Benford, Mervyn, *Milestones*, Shire Library, 2002
Campbell, John, *Complete Castling Handbook*, Butterworth-Heinemann 2011
Darwood, Alex & Martin, Paula, *The Milestones of Fife*, East Fife Preservation Societies, 2005
Fothergill, George A., *British Fire Marks from 1680,* William Green, 1911
Gay, John, *Cast Iron: Architecture and Ornament, Function and Fantasy*, John Murray 1985
Gray, Burton L., *Foundry Work – a Practical Handbook on Standard Foundry Practice. Including Hand and Machine Molding; Cast Iron, Malleable Iron, Steel and Brass Casting, Foundry Management; Etc.* American Technical Society, 1916
Hand, Louis Henry, *Pattern Making and Foundry Practice,* F. J. Drake, 1905
Hands, Stuart, *Road Signs*, Shire Library, 2005
Hasluck, Paul N., *The Pattern Maker's Handybook,* Crosby, Lockwood & Son, 1887
Horner, Joseph Gregory, *Pattern Making, A Practical Treatise*, Crosby, Lockwood & Son, 1885
Horner, Joseph Gregory, *The Principles of Pattern Making written specially for apprentices and students in technical schools,* 1903.
Inglis, J. G., *Engineering Department Instructions*, Great Western Railway, 1898
Owen, Michael, *Antique Cast Iron*, Blandford Press, 1977
Ritchey, James, *Pattern Making – a Manual of Practical Instruction in the use of Woodworking Tools and Machinery. The Making of Simple and Built-up Patterns, and Methods of Molding,* Technical World Magazine 1908
Robertson, Graeme E., *Cast Iron Decoration: A World Survey,* Thames & Hudson, 1977
Shelley, Joseph A., *Pattern Making: A Treatise on the Construction and Application of Patterns*, The Machinery Publishing Company, 1920
Smiles, Samuel, *Industrial Biography*, John Murray, 1862
Whitehouse, P. B. (Editor), *Railway Relics and Regalia,* Country Life, 1975
Williams, Bertram, *Fire Marks and Insurance Office Fire Brigades,* Charles and Edwin Taylor 1927

INDEX

A Treatise on Roads, Parnell, Henry Brooke Parnell 56
A Treatise on the Construction and Application of Patterns 31
Ackermann, Rudolph 87-8
Albion Motor Car Company 68, 71
Alley & McLellan Ltd. 80
Amberley Museum, Sussex 32
Argyll Motors 68, 71
Armstrong, Mitchell & Company 4-5
Armstrong, Sir W. G. & Company 78
Armstrong Whitworth 79, 85
Ashworth & Parker 9
Avoncroft Museum, Bromsgrove 32

Barclay, Andrew, Sons & Company 19, 110
Barlow, William 70
Barrow Hill Roundhouse 105, 115, 119
Beamish The Living Museum of the North 87-8, 119
Beckton Gas Works 31
Bell & Smart, London 19
'Bentomix' Casting sand 44-5
Bergius Launch and Engine Company (Kelvin Diesels) 80
Bertram, James & Sons 9
Beyer, Peacock & Company Ltd 111
Big Pit – the National Coal Museum of Wales 119
Black Clawson company 9
Blaenavon Iron Works 7, 119
Blair, Eric (George Orwell) plaque to 17
Blériot, Louis 71
Bolton Steam Museum 118-120
Brindley, James 73, 76
Bristol Floating Harbour 120
British Celanese Ltd 105
British Motor Museum, Gaydon 50-51, 71, 120
British Railways 98-9, 104, 106
Brunel, Isambard Kingdm 70, 77
Blériot, Louis 29
Bringewood Ironworks 15
Brown, John, Shipyard Clydebank 75
Brunel, Isambard Kingdom 25, 27, 79, 81
Burt, George and Henry, Foundry, Devizes 53-5
Bury, Curtis & Kennedy 92
Burton, Decimus 59
Burrington Churchyard 14-15, 128
Bursledon Brickworks 120

Caen Hill Locks 76, 120
Caledonian Railway 110
Carson & Miller, Warminster 53, 61-2

Caslon, William 93
Casting processes 43-8
Casting sand 37
Chasewater Railway 104
Chemin de Fer Touristique du Haut Quercy
Cholsey & Wallingford Railway 103, 115-6, 120
Christchurch Tramway, New Zealand 25
Claverton Pumping Station 79, 121
Clifton Suspension Bridge 70
Clydebank 75
Coalbrookdale 16, 121
Coldharbour Mill, Devon 24
Colonel Stephens Museum, Tenterden 37, 102, 107, 121
Cope, Sherwin & Company 26
Cornwall, Duchy of 44
Cowans Sheldon & Company 105
Craigellachie Bridge 34-5
Crofton Pumping Station, Wiltshire 24
Crossley Ltd. 80
Cupar Mills Foundry 64-5

Dalglish, Robert, Haigh Foundry Wigan 53
Danks, Fred Ltd 24
Darby Abraham III 16
Devizes & Roundway War Memorial 6
Didcot Railway Centre 67, 87, 94, 107, 111, 113-4, 121
Dinorwig, National Slate Museum of Wales 38-9
Dock, Kerr & Company 31
Dodman, A. & Company 102
Donkin, Bryan 9
Donkin & Company 85
Douglas, Robert, Engineer, Cupar Mills Foundry 64-5
Dove, James 82
Dredge, James 25, 27-9
Drewry Car Company, The 105
Dundas Aqueduct 74
Durn Mill, ittleborough 20

Eagle Forge & Foundry Company, Birmingham 32
Earnshaw & Ho;t, Rchdale 20
East Somerset Railway 107, 121
Ellesmere Canal 35, 78
Ellesmere Port 73, 78
Emerson, Walker & Thompson Brothers Ltd 83
England, George 93
English Heritage 49, 61

Fairbairn, William 18, 80

INDEX

Fakenham Town Gasworks Museum 27, 121
Ffestiniog & Welsh Highland Railway 103, 105
Fire Fly locomotive 91
Forestry England's Westonbirt, The National Arboretum 48-9
Formby, George, plaque to 39
Fothergill, George Algernon 13
Fowler, John & Company 30
Frogmore Paper Mill 9, 122
Fullerton, Hodgart & Barclay Ltd 79
Furness Railway 92, 111

Galloways Ltd, Manchester 24-5
Gayle Mill, Hawes 17, 122
Garretts of Leiston 2-3
Giant Cantilever Crane, Clydebank 75
Gilbert Gilkes & Gordon 17
Gill, Eric 93, 95
Gooch, Daniel 91
Grahame-White, Claude 29
Grangemouth Iron Wrks 55
Great Central Railway 103
Great Eastern Railway 67
Great Northern Railway 115
Great Western Railway 5, 46, 86-7, 90-91, 94-5, 101, 103, 106, 111-112
Great Western Trust, Didcot 67, 87, 94
Green sand 37
Gresley, Nidel 26
Griffin & Company, Bath 31
Guttenberg, Johannes 18
Gray, William & Company, West Hartlepool 83
Great Western Railway (GWR) 46, 74, 79, 86-7, 90-94, 99, 102, 104, 107-112, 116
Great Western Steamship Company 81
GWR Swindon Works 46, 91, 94, 101, 107

Hackwrth, Timothy 89
Haden & Co, Warminster 17
Haigh Foundry, Wigan 53
Hand in Hand Fire & Life Insurance Society 13
Hand, L. H. *Pattern Making & Foundry Practice* 39
Harecastle Tunnel 73
Hasluck, Paul N. *The Pattern Maker's Handybook* 39
Hatcham Iron Works 93
Hawkshaw, John 70
Hazledine, William 17, 34-5, 57
Heidelberg printing machines 8
Highlands End Holiday Park 22-3, 122
Highway Code, The 67
Horner, Joseph G. *Principles of Pattern Making written specially for apprentices and students* 40
HMS *Alliance* 84-5
HMS *M.33 (Minerva)* 85
HMS *Warrior* 82
Humphreys & Oakes 6
Hunslet Engine Company, The 100
Hurst, Nelson & Company Ltd 111

Inglis, James Charles 104, 107-9
Institution of Civil Engineers 57
Iron Duke locomotive 91

Jessop, William 74
Johnston, Edward 93
Jones n Co Cast Metal Designs Ltd 43-5, 48

Jones, Turner & Evans, Newton-le-Willows

Keighley & Worth Valley Railway 100
Kelvin Diesels 80
Kennet and Avon Canal 74-6, 79
Kent & East Sussex Railway 37, 102, 107

Lakeside & Haverthwaite Railway 113, 122
Lancashire Dynamo & Motor Company 75
Lancashire & Yorkshire Railway 99-100, 110
Leeds and Liverpool Canal 75, 77-8
Lion locomotive 89
Lion Salt Works 24
Liverpool & Manchester Railway 88-9
Lobnitz & Company, Renfrew 85
Locomotion No.1 88-9
London General Omnibus Company 67
London, Midland & Scottish Railway (LMS) 95-7, 103
London & North Eastern Railway (LNER) 96-7, 103
London & North Western Railway 77, 93, 95, 99, 101, 111-2
London & South Western Railway 111
Lord, William 24
Lord Street Iron Works, Bury 24

Macfarlane, Walter & Company 36
McNaught, J. W. & Company 118-9
Manchester Liverpool Road Station 93
McGregor, John & Co., Dunedin 83
McGrouther, James 55
Marshall, Thomas J. 26
Marshall, Sns & Company, Gainsborough 30
Mary Rose, warship 11
Mears & Stainbank, Whitechapel 84-5
Merryweather & Sons 22-3, 122
Metallic Label Works 7, 35, 48
Midland Railway 103, 105, 111
Mid-Hants Railway 115, 122
Millennium Mileposts 10-11
Mills, John, sculptor 10-11
Milne, James & Son 9
Motor Cars Acts 37, 67
Motor Rail & Transport Company, The 104
Muirhead, Peter 55

National Collection of Telephone Kiosks, Avoncroft 32
National Railway Museum 92, 123
National Cycle Network 10-11
National Museum of the Royal Navy 122
National Slate Museum Wales 123
National Waterways Museum 123
Neil, J. J. & Company 24
Neilson, Reid & Company 41
Newcomen, Thomas 19
Newport Transporter Bridge 27
North British Locomotive Company Ltd 110
North Norfolk Railway 99
North Star locomotive 91
Norwich Union Fire Insurance Society 13

Orwell, George (Eric Blair) plaque to 39

Parish Boundary markers 33
Park Foundry, Belper 31
Parnell, Henry Brooke *A Treatise on Roads* 56
Pattern Making & Foundry Practice L. L. Hand 39

Peppercorn, Arthur 102
Phoenix Insurance Company 13
Pitman, Sir Isaac & Son 30
Pollitt & Wigzell 30
Pooley, Henry & So 113-4
Portsmouth Historic Dockyard 11, 82, 85, 123
Principles of Patter Making written specially for apprentices and students 40
Pryke & Palmer 67-8
PS *Kingswear Castle* 85
PS *Wingfield Castle* 83

Radstock Museum of Somerset Coalfield Life 74, 123
Railway Act 1903 37
Railway Clearing House 42
Ransome, Sims & Jefferies Ltd 21
Rennie, John 74, 76, 79
Rhymney Railway 40-42, 93
Road Traffic Act 1930 68
Rocket locomotive 89
Roberts, Charles & Company Ltd 103
Robey Trust, The 124
Royal Label Factory 7, 35, 48-9
Royal Train 32-3
Royal Yacht *Britannia* 84-5
Russell, Alex., Kirkcaldy 61, 63

Sankey Canal 77
Sans Pareil locomotive 89
Saracen Foundry, Glasgow 36
Savage, Frederick & Company, King's Lynn 21, 23
Saxon, George 37
Schneider et Cie. 117
Scott & Hodgson, Manchester 30
Sentinel Waggon Works 116
Sharp, Stewart & Company 92
Shelley, Joseph A. *A Treatise on the Construction and Application of Patterns* 41-2
Shropshire Union Canal 78
Shropshire Union Railway & Canal Company 77
Smith & Hawkes 32
Société Alsacienne de Constructions Mécaniques (SACM) 117
Société Générale des Chemins de Fer Econmiques 117 117
Societé des Moteurs Gnome 29
Somerset County Council 69
Somerset & Dorset Joint Railway 111, 113-4
Somersetshire Coal Canal 74-5
Sopwith Aircraft Company 29
South African Railways 110
Southern Railway 2-3, 95, 99, 103, 110, 114
South Oxford Canal 76
SS *Great Britain* steamship 77, 79, 81, 123
SS *Shieldhall* 82, 85, 123

St. George's Churchyard, Burrington 14-15, 120
St. Helens Canal 77
St. Helens & Runcorn Gap Railway 77
STEAM Museum of the Great Western Railway 91, 101, 124
Stockton & Darlington Railway 88
Stephenson, George 89
Stevenson, Robert 82, 89, 91
Stephenson, Robert & Hawthorne Ltd 97
Stothert & Pitt, Bath 18, 75, 80
Stott, S. S. & Co 21
Strathspey Railway 124
Sumburgh Head 80, 124
Summerlee Museum of Scottish Industrial Life 36
Summerlee Museum of Scottish Industrial Life 124
Sun Fire Office 13
Swanage Railway 106, 124

Taff Valley Railway 93
Telephone Kiosks 32
Telford, Thomas 16-17, 25, 34-5, 55-7, 74
The Pattern Maker's Handybook Paul N. Hasluck 39
Thorowgood, William, & Company 95
Titfield Thunderbolt, The, film 89
Tower Bridge, London 4-5, 124
Trencherfield Mill, Wigan 20, 125
Trent & Mersey Canal 72-3
Troup, Francis William 6
TSS *Earnslaw* 83
Turnpike Act, 1706 52
Turnpike Trusts 53, 59-60
Tyer & Company Ltd. 80

Underfall Yard Engine House, Bristol 79

Vulcan Foundry Ltd 100

Wallace (Glasgow) Ltd. 33
Wallis & Steevens Ltd 21
Walschaerts, Egide, valve gear 41
Ward & Silver foundry 17
Watson, Alex. and John, St. Andrews 63
Wessex Archaeology 61
Westonzoyland Pumping Station Museum of Steam Power and Land Drainage 24, 125
West Somerset Railway 99
Whitehead, Harold 30
Whitemill Bridge, Sturminster Marshall 36-7
Wigan Coal & Iron Company 97
Wilkinson Brothers, Kendal 17
Wills, W. & F., Bridgwater 25
Wood, J. & E., Ltd 20
Wood, John & Co 21
Wookey Hole Paper Mill 26, 125